ROUTLEDGE LIBRARY
SHAKESPEARE IN PERFORMANCE

Volume 6

ACTING SHAKESPEARE

ACTING SHAKESPEARE

BERTRAM JOSEPH

Routledge
Taylor & Francis Group

LONDON AND NEW YORK

First published in 1960

This edition first published in 2014
by Routledge
2 Park Square, Milton Park, Abingdon, Oxfordshire OX14 4RN

and by Routledge
711 Third Avenue, New York, NY 10017

First issued in paperback 2016

Routledge is an imprint of the Taylor & Francis Group, an informa business

© 1960, 1969 Bertram Joseph

British Library Cataloguing in Publication Data
A catalogue record for this book is available from the British Library

ISBN: 978-1-138-78774-2 (Set)
ISBN 13: 978-1-138-96586-7 (pbk) (Volume 6)
ISBN 13: 978-1-138-79269-2 (hbk) (Volume 6)

Publisher's Note
The publisher has gone to great lengths to ensure the quality of this book but points out that some imperfections from the original may be apparent.

Disclaimer
The publisher has made every effort to trace copyright holders and would welcome correspondence from those they have been unable to trace.

ACTING

SHAKESPEARE

by

BERTRAM JOSEPH

THEATRE ARTS BOOKS

First published 1960
by Theatre Arts Books
333 Sixth Avenue, New York, N.Y. 10014
Second Impression 1962
Third Impression 1966
Second Edition 1969

© *Bertram Joseph 1960*
Copyright © *1969 by Bertram Joseph*
Library of Congress Catalog Card No. 77–79132
First published as TAB Paperback No. 22, 1969

*I am happy to make acknowledgements to Mr. Peter Selby and
Mr. Angus McBean for leave to publish photographs. I am
indebted to Mr. David Newman for photographs of Miss Shepherd,
and to Theatre Arts Books and Max Reinhardt Ltd. for
permission to quote from* Building a Character
by Constantin Stanislavski.

Printed in the United States of America

To
the memory of
FRANKLYN KELSEY
1891–1958

Bernard Miles as Macbeth.

CONTENTS

ILLUSTRATIONS

FRONTISPIECE

Bernard Miles as Macbeth

BETWEEN PAGES

96 AND 97

Josephine Wilson as Lady Macbeth

Bernard Miles as Macbeth

Elizabeth Shepherd as Juliet

The frontispiece and the picture of Josephine Wilson are from photographs by Peter Selby. The other two of Bernard Miles are by Angus McBean and the three studies of Elizabeth Shepherd are by David Newman

FOREWORD TO THE
SECOND EDITION

SINCE THE FIRST EDITION of this book went to the printer in 1959, I have widened and deepened my experience as a teacher of professional acting students and as a director of professional performances on stage, recordings and film. The fundamental points of theory and practice put forward then have been confirmed by this experience, but I have come to perceive that some additional advice can be given to ensure that the best use be made of the book. One result of editing *Macbeth* for performance and of directing professional actors in the play, has been a change in my view of the Thane. I did not give full attention to his tough ability to accept a reverse, to adjust to it, regather his powers and fight back fiercely with unimpaired vigour. I believe that this heroic quality of Macbeth has been appropriately treated in tape recordings and a set of teaching films for which I have been responsible in the last few years.[1]

In the light of these experiences I am of the opinion that it is impossible to lay too much emphasis on the need for the actor of Shakespeare to play a character with full realization of that character's objectives, whatever else he may be doing. This means that he must be sure of the sense of every word; for only from a clear understanding of the exact sense of every word can he understand the role's intention which is

[1] *The Art of Shakespeare*, 3M Co. (1965); *Shakespeare and Character*, 3M Co. (1966); *Shakespeare and Imagery*, 3M Co. (1966); *Shakespeare's Art in Macbeth*, Films and Guide Book, L. W. Singer Co. (1968).

ix

essential to playing it. For instance, when Lear declares of Cordelia, 'So young and so untender' (I.i.105), the player cannot know his intention without knowing that here the word has the Elizabethan sense of 'stiff, unbending'. It would be a mistake to play a man objecting to harshness or lack of affection in our modern sense of *untender*; Lear wants his daughter to bend, to give way; if he cannot bend her, he is ready to break her, and for that very reason he conducts Burgundy through a sham negotiation, simply in order to show her that without his lands and money she is not wanted. When an actor plays Lear's desire to make her yield, the actress finds that her retort, 'So young, my lord, and true', lets her play the objective of not yielding and of asserting that honesty makes her refuse to; she is 'dead straight'.

To play his role, attempting to attain the character's objective in action, the actor must beware of many temptations which may unobtrusively divert him. Familiarity may hide from a Hamlet the fact that in the first soliloquy he does not yet suspect his uncle of murder and wants simply to speak out and open everybody's eyes to what he sees happening. He is sure that if he tried, he would fail to convince anyone: 'But break my heart, for I must hold my tongue.' Sometimes the beauty of imagery or sound tempts us to forget the intention. Edgar's description of the cliff as he imagines it will succeed only if the actor plays a man determined to convince his blind father that they are so many feet above sea (IV.vi,11–24). Titania's account of the unnaturally inclement weather in *A Midsummernight's Dream* (II.1.81–117) must not be spoken as a beautiful piece of description; her intention is to win her battle with her husband. The actress has to remember the wet months as if she experienced not only her distress for the mortals, but her discontent during all this time because her husband has been adamant. Now she aims at making him see that their strife is responsible for the weather, that if they were reconciled the damage would end, and that they could easily be reconciled if he would only yield to her. Every word which she utters is a reproach because he has been so unpleasant and will not humour her. A shorter, but similar example occurs with the famous line of the First Murderer in *Macbeth*: 'the west yet glimmers with some streaks of day'. He has been commanded strictly by Macbeth to kill Banquo and Fleance in secret without being seen coming to or leaving the ambush. This means he must not take up position until it is dark enough not to be seen. When he gets there he wonders if he is too late; to make sure he looks in the west and sees with satisfaction that there is some daylight left. That is his reason for the statement. His objective is to wait in ambush and kill his unsuspecting victims.

There is danger of being diverted from the main task of playing the role's objective in such famous descriptive pieces as Gertrude's account of Ophelia's death. Here the intention is to prevent Laertes from being too violently affected. Partly because she feels for him, partly because she does not want him to burst out in fresh opposition, Gertrude concentrates on assuring him that this is how it happened: his sister fell by accident into the water, whereupon her clothes spread out holding her upright, from her waist up out of the water like a mermaid as she sang. Obviously, Gertrude insists, she had no idea of her danger; there was no anguish as in her crazed delight she floated down the stream until suddenly, all in a moment, her clothes became saturated and their weight dragged her swiftly under. The emphasis is on the pathetic peace and happiness of the girl who made no attempt to save herself simply because she had no idea of her danger. Whether Gertrude believes this or not, her intention is to convince Laertes that this is exactly what happened, so that he is not too overcome both for his own sake and hers and her husband's. Similarly Enobarbus's intention in his famous description of Cleopatra is to let his Roman friends know just what she is like; he remembers the scene, how he felt, his amusement at Antony's discomforture, his awareness that this woman is a force to be reckon ed with; he wants these Romans to realize what they have to deal with, how strong is her hold on Antony, how great is the danger that Octavia will not be able to satisfy him after his Egyptian love (II.ll.194–209).

Chapters One and Two call attention to details of Shakespeare's style and thus to aspects of technique in acting. If these chapters are to do most good and no harm they must be used with every effort to recognize how stylistic details communicate the intention of the character; these must be played so as to communicate that intention. The figures of speech are not an end in themselves; their intricacy must not divert the actor from playing a character in action so as to achieve his objective.[1]

At all times it is essential to realize that Shakespeare uses words very precisely; however rich the imagery, powerful the emotion and intention, it will be found that he has written very precise surface sense. It is necessary to *think* this sense if each word is to be articulated as part of a coordinated verbal and non-verbal communication of meaning in the attempt to achieve an objective in relation to other persons or to forces which help or obstruct.

This account of acting Shakespeare is based in many respects upon the methods of Elizabethan actors. The fact that much of our knowledge of their art has come from what is said of it in descriptions of the sister art of 'oratory' sometimes causes confusion. I have dealt with the relationship fully elsewhere.[2] Here it is enough to point out that the Elizabethan actor identified himself with a role, and the orator identified himself with the person or situation he was describing; both used voice and body to communicate emotion, thought and the want to obtain an objective. The Elizabethan was taught in school to use private images to

[1]The recordings mentioned above illustrate this point.
[2]*Elizabethan Acting* (2nd Ed. 1964), Oxford University Press.

evoke emotion. He took the actor as his model. It would be more accurate to say that what the Elizabethans called oratory was in fact the art of verbal and non-verbal communication of meaning by voice and body. The Elizabethans often speak of 'external action', not because they made the mistake of ignoring inner reality, but because the world had not yet experienced the Cartesian fallacy of what Gilbert Ryle has called 'the ghost in the machine'. They knew that external action and inner reality were one and the same thing. Professor Duncan Ross has recently called attention to the consequences of the Cartesian separation of mind and body in leading Stanislavski astray in his account of his work but not the work itself.[1]

To sum up, what is good acting outside Shakespeare is good acting in Shakespeare, all that is different is the play. The actor's difficulties do not arise from what has to be done or how, but in recognizing the demands which Shakespeare makes on him which are often disguised by the qualities of his text. This book is an attempt to explain the demands and to suggest some of the ways to meet them.

BERTRAM JOSEPH
University of Washington,
Seattle 1969

[1] *Towards an Organic Approach to Actor Training*, Educational Theatre Journal, Special Issue (August 1968) pp. 238 ff.

PREFACE

FROM THE VERY EARLY DAYS of preparing this book I
have been fortunate enough to have had the comment and
advice of Mr. Bernard Miles and his wife, Miss Josephine
Wilson, both of whom have added to my debt of gratitude
by their readiness to put suggestions to a practical test, in
productions at the Mermaid Theatre between 1951 and
1953, and in private since. Mr. Geoffrey Taylor has similarly helped with his interest and his talent since our
meeting at the Mermaid in 1952. To no one do I owe more
gratitude than to these three.

Helpful discussion and advice have come from Professor
W. Beare, Mr. G. Brandt, Mr. C. Tomlinson and Dr. J.
Wilders, my colleagues in the University of Bristol. I am
also indebted to Mr. John Andrew of St. Catharine's College,
Cambridge, Dr. W. A. Armstrong of King's College,
London, Professor A. G. H. Bachrach of the University of
Leiden, Dr. P. Brockbank of the University of Reading,
Mr. C. J. A. Hill, of Redland Training College, to Mr.
W. A. Darlington, Mr. Peter Howell, Mr. Kenneth Hudson,
Mr. Eric Robinson of the City of Coventry Training College,
and to Mr. Noel Thomas.

The following have been kind enough to read one part or
another of the typescript while it was in preparation and to
help immeasurably with their knowledge and encouragement: Mr. E. Martin Browne, Professor Nevill Coghill,
Mr. Peter Coe, Dr. Tyrone Guthrie, Miss Joan Littlewood,
Miss Yvonne Mitchell, Mr. Gerald Raffles, Mr. Tony

Richardson, Mr. John Stevens, Mr. and Mrs. J. C. Trewin.

I feel happy to acknowledge the immense assistance I have received from teaching this subject for some years in the Bristol Old Vic Theatre School. A special word of thanks is due to Duncan Ross, the Principal, and to my colleagues, Margaret Collins, Daphne Heard, William Moore and Rudi Shelly. More recently I have had a similar experience teaching in the London Academy of Music and Dramatic Art at the invitation of its Principal, Mr. Michael Mac-Owan, who has long given me his informed interest and encouragement. I am indebted to Dr. Hilda Hulme for her explanation of the meaning of 'trammel', and to an article by Mr. W. M. Merchant in *Shakespeare Quarterly,* Vol. IX (1958), for the information on Poussin and Hayman as illustrators of *Coriolanus.*

Finally I have to record my very deep gratitude for the inspiration afforded to me by that magnificent teacher, the late Mr. Franklyn Kelsey, who first made me realize fully what the human voice is capable of in speech as well as song.

Bristol, September, 1959.   B. L. J.

INTRODUCTION

TO SOME EXTENT the title of this book may easily be misleading. For, while it is certainly concerned with acting Shakespeare, it does not presume to tell anybody what to do while acting on the stage. Instead, the pages which follow contain suggestions which it is hoped may be useful to those engaged in preparing a Shakespearian role; and these suggestions are made by one who is very conscious of the difference between preparing a role and acting it.

Everything that is put forward here has been found of use in practice, either in preparation for actual productions at the Mermaid Theatre when it was in St. John's Wood and the Royal Exchange, or in exercises and in the preparation of roles at the Bristol Old Vic Theatre School and at the London Academy of Music and Dramatic Art. Experience has led me to believe that there is probably nobody who will need to make use of everything in the book; on the other hand, the same experience suggests that there is nothing in it which will be entirely valueless to everybody. Yet it is equally certain that there are many people who will find that the suggestions made here are not needed, because they have already developed their own individual methods of overcoming the difficulties discussed.

It should be made clear from the start that this is no attempt to sell a method or a system; of necessity, system must be used in the presentation of the material, but the last thing which is desired is that on this account it should be thought that these suggestions are advocated as an indis-

pensable panacea for all the ills that can afflict the Shakespearian actor. One hope has certainly been present all the
time, that the book may help to attain the end for which all
strive, performances which satisfy the artistic conscience of
the actor: and to that end certain aspects of Elizabethan
practice and theory have been analysed to find equivalent
ways of satisfying modern actors and audiences.

It is often suggested that what the modern English
theatre needs is to develop a Shakespearian 'style'. I would
prefer to say that what is really needed is a different understanding of Shakespeare's style of dramatic writing, so that
his unrealistic use of his medium does not impede and in-
hibit, but actually helps the actor anxious to recognize and
express the emotions and purposes of the imaginary character. For the actor, rightly, knows that whatever may be said
about Shakespearian themes and poetry, his task is to create
character.

It is the author's belief, indeed, that the actor's task is
simply nothing more than the truthful creation of character
as completely as the dramatist requires. But when the
dramatist is Shakespeare, the actor can only carry out this
task when he gives attention to aspects of the plays often
regarded as literary rather than dramatic. But this dicho-
tomy is indeed false; for on the one hand, the poetic quality
of the lines can be fully realized only when they are spoken
in character; yet, on the other, the completely imagined and
truthful character can itself be realized only when the
qualities of the literary text are taken into account at some
stage of preparation.

In the pages which follow a great deal of time is spent
calling attention to the way in which Shakespeare has
imagined his characters in the medium of words, used in a
highly specialized way. This may lead to an impression that
lines are analysed here in order to direct the actor's attention away from his main task, the creation of character. But
in fact, provided he remembers that such analysis is no more

than a means to the end of creating the character, the actor will find that this, like other conscious elements of preparation, recedes into its proper place in the background of his mind when he is acting. For instance, he may not think consciously of using the figure, antithesis, when the opposition of contraries which are contained in the sense of a passage, and in the character's emotion and purpose, will necessarily come to external expression in his acting because they must.

While the primary aim of the book is to suggest ways of preparing to act, this preparation, as has been observed, involves a type of analysis not unlike that associated with literary criticism and the appreciation of verse. As a result it may well be objected that it is possible to appreciate Shakespeare's art without the close analysis undertaken here. This is, of course, absolutely true; but the purpose of the book is not to make suggestions which will lead to a better appreciation of Shakespeare's poetry; the purpose is to suggest ways of preparing to act which will help actors to overcome difficulties which actually exist for them today. The analysis is suggested as part of the preparation for acting a role and not as part of a system of the appreciation of literature.

A note is needed also as to the way in which passages have been chosen for analysis and comment. They are not put forward in order to prove anything about Shakespeare's art. Their purpose is simply to illustrate the kind of problems to be found in Shakespeare with a suggestion as to the way in which these problems may be solved. And if it were to prove on inquiry that sometimes I have chosen examples which are unique and not to be found anywhere else in his work, that does not by any means affect the validity of the principles on which I am working; for the fact that a problem occurs no more than once does not mean that it does not occur at all. And if we have found a solution to it where it occurs, we can pass on all the more attentively to other difficulties which are more widespread. For the aim and method of the book is to call attention to the nature of difficulties where they exist, and not to argue that all difficulties are like those analysed, and that therefore all can be cured in the same way. There is more to the acting of Shakespeare than is dealt with in this book; but everything that is dealt with is nevertheless vitally involved in acting him at some time or another. To treat the whole of Shakespeare's works along the lines suggested here would obviously be impracticable in a publication. For that reason there has to be a selection of examples: and in the last chapter, on character, I have given fairly detailed treatment to Juliet, Friar Lawrence and Macbeth. The two first have been chosen because Shakespeare's language is obviously very unrealistic in their cases, and because with them the figures are often so obtrusive as to be an obstacle to the modern performer: on the other hand, Macbeth's lines are unrealistic in a somewhat different way, with figures which the modern tends not to notice, but which contribute much to Shakespeare's, and thus to the actor's, full imagining of the character to be portrayed.

A work which devotes so much attention to examples of the figures in Shakespeare's dialogue provokes the question, how far did his technique in this respect change with the development of his art as a whole? It may also be wondered if it is possible to demonstrate how he differed from other dramatists in his use of figures, and whether his example influenced them. Obviously these are valid questions; but no attempt has been made to answer them here. To some extent this is because I do not feel qualified to make the attempt; but an even stronger reason lies in the fact that this book is not aimed at evaluating Shakespeare's art, nor that of his contemporaries, but simply at considering problems which he offers to modern actors, and ways of overcoming these problems.

Finally the point is emphasized that what is written in

the pages which follow is never hesitant, but always tentative: never hesitant, because the best way to prove a suggestion is to make it and let it stand the test of practice;
always tentative, because the test of practice may (and often
does) show fallacies and suggest modifications.

One

THE SCHOOLBOY AND
THE ACTOR

IT IS EASY ENOUGH for an actor playing Shakespeare to create a character so completely that he seems to be the very man whom he is impersonating. But the same modern actor finds it much more difficult to act as completely in character, and yet contrive to speak the lines in such a way that the audience can be stirred by all those details of the poetry which we can enjoy when we have the words in front of us on the printed page. Actors who have not acquired the art of doing both these things may still satisfy us with their ability to make an imaginary character come to life, but only so long as we are ready to miss in the theatre much of that poetry which we find in Shakespeare when we read him for ourselves.

That this should be the case is unfortunate, for while Shakespeare is a powerful dramatist, he is no less a superb poet; and it is even possible to argue, and to demonstrate, that the person who does not respond to his plays fully as poetry is at the same time unable to respond to them fully as drama. Shakespeare has not merely imagined his characters, invented his plots and pondered their themes and implications as plays; the art which he exercises as a poet in his sonnets and his narrative poems is the art which he retains with the same full liberty in his tragedies, his

1

comedies and his histories. For Shakespeare there is no conflict between the demands of poetry and those of drama; in
his plays the two are one; and to enjoy him to the full as a
dramatist we must be moved by the way in which he uses
language as a poet; the converse is no less true, of course,
that to enjoy him completely as a poet in his plays, we must
also be moved by him as a dramatist. The result is that the
actor who does not allow us to experience Shakespeare as a
poet in the theatre keeps from us an essential of his art: but
the actor who understands thoroughly the way in which
Shakespeare is working purely as a poet in imagining and
expressing the feelings and wishes of his characters will find
that he has acquired a knowledge which will not only let him
speak the lines as poetry, but which will aid him at the same
time in giving the pure breath of life to his impersonation.

For the fact is that with Shakespeare for the most part
character and poetry are so inseparable that a failure to
communicate the poetic quality will be accompanied by a
failure to penetrate the living depths of the character. But a
study of the details of the lines and of their structure leads
straight into those depths. Indeed, this plea to give Shakespeare as a poet in the theatre is justified only, yet more
than adequately, by the simple fact that anything else that
an actor may do when this playwright's lines come from
his mouth, stirring, exciting and dramatic as it may be, is
not so stirring, exciting and dramatic as communicating
their poetic quality; in that lies the best of good theatre.

The plea made here is not for literature rather than
drama. No solution of the problem of acting Shakespeare
today is to be found in giving what is often called a 'beautifully spoken', but is in fact a comparatively undramatic,
performance of a play. No undramatic performance can
really be beautifully spoken, for the sound of living emotion
which comes from complete identification with the character in the imagined situation is an element essential to the
real beauty of spoken Shakespeare. Without this element

the lines are pale and emasculate. If I were asked to choose between an 'unpoetical' performance which was at least good theatre, and one which was 'poetical' at the expense of the play's dramatic qualities, I would invariably choose good theatre. It is possible, however, to have the best theatre together with the most beautiful poetry when the actor's preparation of his part has been based on a clear recognition of the way in which his lines have been constructed as units of verse and prose.

That verse-speaking should be based on an understanding of the structure of the verse seems obvious enough: but what is not so plainly recognized today is that when an actor sees clearly the way in which a passage is built up as an organized relationship of words and sounds, he has also gained an insight into the character of the speaker as that was imagined by the author. This insight, essential to the complete impersonation of that imagined character, can, after all, only be obtained from its creator's words, and the dialogue or monologue in which its imagined thoughts and emotions are expressed. For instance, an understanding of Shakespeare's art as a poet is necessary for the actor who wants to identify himself with Henry V in the scene in which the King sends the French ambassadors back to their master with an answer to the insulting gift of tennis-balls. When he orders them to go back to France and tell their Prince what repercussions 'this mock of his' will have on their country, the actual choice and arrangement of the words emphasize the quality of Henry's resentment; they reveal the controlled intelligence which Shakespeare has imagined uttering a powerful threat without this intimidating anger degenerating into the boastfulness of arrogance:

> for many a thousand widows
> Shall this his mock mock out of their dear husbands;
> Mock mothers from their sons, mock castles down;
>
> (HENRY V, I, ii, 284–6)

3

In patterning sounds and rhythms in these lines to carry sense and to express character and situation, Shakespeare has repeated the word 'mock' four times, but not always with the same meaning. The Dauphin's mock will mock widows out of their dear husbands; it will mock mock mothers who have lost their sons; it will also mock down mock castles. And each repetition of the word, when given with meaning, comes as a fresh blow, not unlike the sound of a tennis-ball when it is struck. Thus has the playwright imagined Henry replying ironically to the Dauphin's humour with the promise of grimmer things, this section of the speech closing with the rhyming couplet:

> And some are yet ungotten and unborn
> That shall have cause to curse the Dauphin's scorn.

An understanding of Shakespeare's art here enables the actor to make full use of the near-rhyme 'cause to curse' as the irony is capped in a sardonic full-close. And then he finds himself resenting the insult and looking forward to wiping it out with that grim and dangerous humour which is part of the full characterization of Shakespeare's king.

To have recognized the details which we have just been considering, and to have understood their importance, an Elizabethan would have needed no greater knowledge than was offered to children at the grammar school. He would have known that the play upon the different uses of the word 'mock' was an example of what was described technically as the rhetorical figure *Atnanaclasis*. In Puttenham's *Art of English Poesie* (1589) this figure is described as 'the Rebound' on account of the way in which it works: and we are told that an arrangement of words of this kind is called 'the Rebound' because it is reminiscent of 'the tennis-ball which being smitten with the racket rebounds back again'.[1]

Here, in *Henry V*, Shakespeare has used the figure of the Rebound to express the appalling consequences which are

[1] Ed. G. D. Willcock and A. Walker (1936), p. 207.

to come in the rebound of the Dauphin's insulting tennis-balls back upon France as gun-stones. If the actor, however, does not speak the words so that an audience can hear and respond to the pattern, he deprives them of something fundamental to Shakespeare's conception of Henry and of his story. And our Elizabethan would not only have recognized the figure and appreciated its use: he would have known how to speak it so that it could function for the audience, so that listeners would have been affected by these comparatively minute details of Shakespeare's poetic technique. This is an extreme case, analagous to Mozart's use of the horn in the orchestra when the Duke deems himself 'cornuto'; and something must have been lost, as it is today, for every member of the audience unable to put a name to the figure of rebound. But no matter how simple the figure, no matter how obvious it may have been to the educated Elizabethan, we today cannot help wondering how much was perceived by the individual members of the audience, and how far did the dramatist expect them to perceive how he was using the figures. To ask these questions, however, presupposes that the figures were used as an end in themselves; whereas the truth seems to be that they were used as any technique is, once it has been mastered, unconsciously, except on those occasions when care is taken over exactly what is to be expressed in that technique. And then the artist's interest is still not in the technique as such, but in exactly what has to be said by means of it. The sense, emotion and purpose were what counted; for an actor to express them in the words used by the poet is to make the figures 'manifest', not as patterns isolated from the rest, but as elements contributing to something larger, with the smaller and the larger primarily an expression of what the character feels and wants. In these circumstances, while educated members of the audience would have an appreciation of technicalities somewhere in their response to a performance, it would not be anything like dominant. And those in the audience who could neither name the figures, nor hear them as such, would still respond to the actor's expression through them of the character's emotion and purpose. A speaker who was not a good actor could still emphasize the words and inflect his voice to bring out the meaning and convey enough of the emotion to show what is going on in Henry's mind. But, of course, for the passage to have its maximum effect, whoever speaks it ought to be identified with the character, sharing Henry's objective, asserting himself to prove that an apparently misspent youth was only the prelude to great deeds, in which moreover he will avenge himself upon the sneering French Prince and impose his will on France. The superficial details of poetic technique reveal fundamental truths of character, helping the actor to clarify his objective.

Elizabethan grammar-school masters spent a good proportion of their time teaching their pupils to perceive clearly the detailed organization of a poet's language, and to use voice and gesture so that the details were not lost to an audience. The boys were taught to recognize the different individual organizations of sound and sense in prose as well as verse: they also learned the names given to these in the standard works on the subject. And the boy who profited from this schooling was able to recognize the figure known as *Paronomasia* when he read the words 'shall have cause to curse'. He knew, as well, that this same figure is involved in Macbeth's longing for assurance that the killing of Duncan will 'catch,/With his surcease, success'. (I, vii, 3–4.) *Paronomasia* is one of those figures known technically as figures of words: and the boy who knew this also knew that Gloucester in *King Lear* is speaking in the pattern of sound and sense called a metaphor, which is technically a trope, when he declares that if he could bear to live longer, his

snuff and loathed part of nature should
Burn itself out.

(IV, vi, 39–40)

One Elizabethan schoolmaster, William Kempe of Plymouth, insists on the general need for his own practice of teaching boys to recognize 'every trope, every figure as well of words as of sentence'.[1] This was, in fact, the general practice in the grammar schools of England in the sixteenth and seventeenth centuries: and it resulted in boys learning not only that metaphor is a trope and paronomasia a figure of words, but that a 'figure of sentence' is one 'which in the whole sentence' expresses 'some motion of the mind', that is, some emotion of the mind.[2] Whoever knew this could not fail to recognize as a figure of sentence the apostrophe of Cleopatra:

> O happy horse, to bear the weight of Antony!
>
> (I, v, 21.)

What is even more important, however, is that the schoolmasters who agreed with Kempe in teaching boys to recognize the figures also shared with him the universal practice of teaching their pupils what he calls 'the rhetorical pronunciation and gesture for every word, sentence and affection (i.e. emotion)'.[3] In other words, they were taught not only to recognize Gloucester's metaphor in *King Lear* as a trope, but, that for the figure to affect an audience, the word 'burn' must be emphasized so that the listeners can realize that the 'snuff and loathed part' is going to be put out suddenly, and will not be left to burn itself out in the normal way. The boys were taught how to emphasize the repetitions of 'mock' and the near-rhymes, 'cause to curse', 'surcease, success', so that these particular ways of using language to express the poet's imagining of the character's wishes would be as effective for the listener as for a reader. Similarly, when the competent Elizabethan speaker came to Cleopatra's apostrophe, he would speak the words addressed

[1] *The Education of Children* (1588), sig. G 3ʳ.
[2] A. Fraunce, *The Arcadian Rhetoric* (1588), ed. Seaton (1950), p. 63.
[3] *Op. cit.*, sig. G 3ʳ.

7

to the horse in her mind's eye with the emotion and in the manner which would be appropriate were she addressing a horse actually in her presence with Antony seated on it.

Hardly a school founded or refounded in England in the sixteenth century omits from its statutes some provision for teaching this art of 'rhetorical pronunciation and gesture'. King's School, Canterbury, where Marlowe was a pupil, insists typically that the boys should be taught 'due decorum both with their body and their mouth'.[1] Despite its somewhat pompous phrasing, this means exactly what Hamlet has in mind with his direction, 'Suit the action to the word, the word to the action.' The aim of the schoolmasters was to give the Elizabethan schoolboy a thorough theoretical grounding and at least competence in the practice of an art which can be very effective when subordinated to the talents of a mature actor.

The art of 'pronunciation' practised in the schools of Shakespeare's England demanded a clear articulation and a well-disciplined voice with flexibility and a good range of tone, volume and intensity; to the modulations of the voice were added a grace of movement which came from perfect control of the body, head and limbs. From a boy's first days in school steps were taken to start him on the systematic drill which would eventually equip him to make of himself an instrument which could embody the exact quality of the words he was speaking, as music and movement, and as meaning.

Clear enunciation was demanded from the very beginning. 'From the first entrance', says John Brinsley in his advice to schoolmasters, the boys should be taught 'to pronounce everything audibly, leisurely, distinctly, and naturally; sounding out specially the last syllable, that each word may be fully understood'.[2] He does not want the last syllable to be exaggerated: he merely wants to make certain

[1] A. F. Leach, *Educational Charters* (1911), p. 467.
[2] *Ludus Literarius: Or The Grammar School* (1612), pp. 50 f.

8

that the boys are not allowed to fall into the slovenly habit of swallowing it. Similarly, Wolsey's instructions to his masters at his refounding of the school at Ipswich insist that even in the first form which contains 'the most ignorant boys' who are learning only the eight parts of speech, 'let your principal attention be to form their tender articulation, so as in a full, elegant tone of voice they may pronounce the elements they are taught; for it is possible to mould their rude materials into any form'. We find the same care asked for when it comes to teaching the fourth form, for which no writer is better than 'Virgil, the Prince of Poets'. It will be well worth the trouble, the instructions run, to make the boys pronounce 'his majestic lines in a deep, full articulation'.[1] And in the schools of the sixteenth century so much was learned by heart and repeated aloud that there was every opportunity for the masters to develop the clear enunciation that is so necessary. It was no more than a normal part of their routine, without any alteration of the curriculum, to carry out such demands as those made in the statutes of Bury St. Edmunds to 'take diligent heed and beware for their scholars' distinct and plain pronunciation'.[2]

At the same time 'diligent heed' was taken that clear and complete articulation should not lead to monotony. 'The boys are not to speak as a boy who is saying his lesson,' says Brinsley.[3] And at Bury St. Edmunds, those who were being instructed 'in the first elements of grammar' were on no account to be allowed 'to utter words at random and without understanding like parrots, but are to pronounce with pleasing and apt modulation, tempered with variety'. When they were once able to speak and read in Latin they should not be allowed to utter words 'without full and perfect understanding of the matter and meaning thereof'. The

[1] T. W. Baldwin, *William Shakespeare's Small Latine & Less Greek* (1944), I, 152.
[2] See Baldwin, *ibid.*, I, 301, 306.
[3] *Op. cit.*, p. 212.

master should see 'that they read not nor speak in one time, but that diligent heed be given to the due accent in pronunciation'.[1]

In his educational treatise, *Positions* (1581), Richard Mulcaster, the famous headmaster of Merchant Taylors' School, gives us a glimpse of the methods which could be used to ensure the development of 'pleasing and apt modulation, tempered with variety'. He describes the exercise called *vociferatio*, or *Loudspeaking* (also known as *Crying-out*), which was designed to develop a range of tone and volume. Those children who could read recited 'either Iambic verses, or Elegies, or other such numbers, which with their current carry the memory on'. It was all to be done as loudly as possible, but not monotonously or without meaning. As for the children who had not yet learned to read, they said 'such things as they could remember, which were to be spoken aloud, and admitted any change of voice in the uttering, now harsh and hard, now smooth and sweet'. And on no account were those who could read to be allowed to use a book: one of the points of the exercise was that it demanded imaginative as well as physical effort. Mulcaster considered this drill to be 'both the first in rank, and the best mean to make good pronouncing of anything, in any auditory, and therefore an exercise not impertinent to scholars'.[2]

By such means boys were taught to articulate clearly, and to modulate the voice flexibly and tunefully: but for what was called 'apt pronunciation' still more was needed, the ability to understand the meaning and structure of a line so that in the delivery, as Hamlet puts it, 'the action' suits 'the word'. For this reason the early exercises which trained enunciation, tone and volume were supplemented later by practice in pronouncing such patterns of language as occur in the passages from Shakespeare examined earlier in this

[1]See Baldwin, I, 306.
[2]pp. 55–58.

chapter. 'Let them also be taught carefully,' says Brinsley, 'in what word the Emphasis lyeth, and therefore which is to be elevated in pronunciation. As namely those words in which the chief Trope or Figure is.'[1]

As soon as the boys had learned enough grammar and the topics of logic a great deal of attention was given to figures and tropes. One collection used in school, the *Epitome* of Susenbrotus, contains the definitions of 132 figures, each with its illustration. Two other works which became almost standard are the *Rhetorica* of Talaeus, and the book by Charles Butler which was based on it and which bore the same name. These two books were each in two parts, the second of which was devoted to pronunciation, giving elementary rules, to which were added actual examples of the figures to be used as exercises. Brinsley recommends 'the second book of Talaeus Rhetoric *de pronunciatione*; or rather of Master Butler's Rhetoric'. To teach boys to act the emotions which the words might happen to express, 'and that they may do everything according to the very nature', he suggests 'acquaint them to pronounce some special examples set down in Talaeus Rhetoric as pathetically (i.e. emotionally) as they can: as examples of Ironies, Exclamations, Revocations, Prosopopeias, and those which are in his rules of pronouncing'.[2]

All this was taught in Latin, but what is substantially the same can be found in English in Abraham Fraunce's *The Arcadian Rhetoric* (1588). Here the different figures are defined and then illustrated by examples of English prose and verse, and in Italian and French as well as in Latin and Greek quotations. Fraunce also gives the usual rules for pronouncing the figures. It goes without saying that he insists on the need for a flexible voice and for grace of movement. When training has been satisfactory, 'by that kind of voice which belongeth to whole sentences, all kinds of

[1] pp. 213 f.
[2] pp. 214; 213.

11

figures and passionate ornaments of speech are made manifest'.

Among the figures which Fraunce defines are those involving the repetitions of the same or similar sounds. He places paronomasia among patterns of 'sounds somewhat unlike', quoting examples from Sir Philip Sidney, one of which runs as follows:

Come shepherds' weeds, *become* your masters' minds.

A second, in prose, is:

But, alas, what can *saying* make them believe, whom *seeing* cannot persuade?

The Elizabethan schoolboy learned definitions and examples such as these in Latin: he also learned that in speaking those figures 'which altogether consist in sweet repetitions and dimensions, is chiefly conversant that pleasant and delicate tuning of the voice which resembleth the consent and harmony of some well ordered song'[1]. It is therefore not surprising that Shakespeare expected his actors to manage to perform Henry V's 'cause to curse' and Macbeth's 'surcease, success' so that the audience was able to respond to his arranging of similar sounds in relationship to one another.

Kempe was conforming to the usual practice when he taught his boys in Plymouth to recognize the tropes and to pronounce them. According to Fraunce a trope is 'when a word is turned from his natural signification, to some other, so conveniently, as that it seem rather willingly led, than driven by force to that other signification. This was first invented of necessity for want of words, but afterwards continued and frequented by reason of the delight and pleasant grace thereof.' He proceeds to define and illustrate the different kinds of such tropes as metonymy, irony, metaphor and synecdoche. Of the tropes Fraunce considers that 'the most

[1] *Op. cit.*, pp. 106 f; 49 f; 107.

12

excellent is Metaphor; the next, Ironia'. And when it comes to pronunciation he declares that 'in the particular applying of the voice to several words, we make tropes that be most excellent plainly appear. For without this change of voice, neither any Ironia, nor lively Metaphor can well be discerned.'[1]

Empty and mechanical 'applying of the voice' to make the tropes 'plainly appear' is obviously not enough, although it may be necessary at some early stage of the preparation. But if the trope is really to affect the listener, all the meaning and emotion which it expresses must be communicated in the speaking; and it is probable that, had Fraunce or his contemporaries been questioned on this point, they would have replied that obviously the trope does not plainly appear unless emotion and meaning inform the 'change of voice' —in fact, that the change of voice is the result of the speaker imagining the meaning and emotion as he speaks. This seems a reasonable assumption taking into account the emphasis which the conventional renaissance treatment of the subject places on the need for identification and for the communication of both the meaning and emotion expressed by means of the figures.

In addition to figures of words and tropes, the learned grammarian had to recognize and pronounce figures of sentence, those which Fraunce defines as expressing some emotion 'in the whole sentence'. Like the schoolmasters he stresses the importance of a delivery which is suited to the different emotions: and he gives examples in which the various passions are expressed, and which are to be acted accordingly. With these 'figures of affections' the voice is 'more manly' than with figures of words, 'yet diversely, according to the variety of passions that are to be expressed'.[2]

Pronunciation in the grammar school made demands upon the speaker very similar to those of play-acting. When-

[1] *Ibid.*, pp. 3 ff.; 106.
[2] *Op. cit.*, p. 107.

ever a text required the imaginative representation of character or emotions, the boys were expected to pronounce it accordingly: and many of the texts used in the grammar school do, in fact, require this kind of speaking. This must be the way, says Brinsley, 'where persons or other things are feigned to speak'. When the boys were taken through the collection of dialogues entitled *Confabiatiunculae Pueriles*, 'cause them to utter every dialogue lively, as if they themselves were the persons which did speak in that dialogue, & so in every other speech, to imagine themselves to have occasion to utter the very same things'.[1] In the upper forms it was usual to follow the practice recommended by Mulcaster of pronouncing 'without book, with that kind of action which the very property of the subject requireth, orations and other declamatory arguments, either made by the pronouncer himself, or borrowed of some other'.[2] This practice has the approval of Brinsley, who also recommends competitive debates in which the boys should 'pronounce themes or declamations, striving who shall do best: and in all their oppositions to dispute as if *ex animo* in good earnest, with all contention and vehemency'. He likes the practice (common to the grammar schools of the period) of 'pronouncing emphatically of some of Tully's Orations' with the right emphasis and action for the meaning and emotion. As these speeches are 'most flowing in figures of sentences (especially in exclamations, prosopopeias, apostrophes, and the like)' they gave good practice. In this manner the boys would become acquainted with 'great variety of pronunciation, to be fitted for all sorts'.[3]

How much practice a boy was given in pronunciation of this sort, in fact, begins to come home to us only when we examine the details of the curriculum which are more or less common to all the grammar schools of the age. The aim

[1] *Op cit.*, p. 212.
[2] *Positions* (1581), p. 55
[3] *Op. cit.*, p. 214

was to make him enunciate clearly, modulate his voice fittingly and act emotion and imagine himself in a speaker's character whenever the opportunity presented itself. Authors such as Terence, Plautus and Virgil, Aesop (in Latin), Ovid, Caesar, Lucan, Horace, Juvenal and Persius, in addition to collections of extracts and of adagia and dialogues were turned into English, and then the translation itself turned back into Latin in each case. As much of the work was oral and had to be learned by heart to be repeated aloud, every boy at school must have been obliged before he left to pronounce shorter or longer passages in English and Latin thousands of times 'according to the very nature of it', and with some attempt at satisfying the universal demand for 'due decorum both with body and with mouth'. But this was not all: the fourteen minor prose themes of Aphthonius were studied before the boys began to make orations: Sallust, Justin, Valerius Maximus, Lucius Florus and Pliny were also read. Then came lessons in writing orations, and these involved the study of the *Rhetorica ad Herenium* and Quintilian's *Institutes*, followed by detailed work on Cicero. Later there was also Greek, the grammar of which was first studied in Latin, with translations of passages from one language to the other; and such texts were eventually read as the New Testament in Greek, Isocrates, Homer, with probably some of Demosthenes, Pindar, Euripides, Plutarch, Theocritus, Hesiod, Xenophon, Dionysius of Halicarnassus, Heliodorus and the epistles of Saint Basil. The cumulative result of all this pronouncing, year in, year out, until a boy left school, must have been that, even if he had little or no talent as an actor, he acquired an understanding of what was involved in the speaking of prose and verse, dramatic or not, if the listeners were to be allowed to respond to the real qualities of what was being spoken.

The final polish to pronouncing was given at the universities and at the inns of court, where, in addition to formal speechifying, the young men acted in plays which gave confidence and demanded the technical ability to use voice and gesture. And plays were put on for the same reasons in the schools. Mulcaster's pupils acted before the Queen, and so did the children of the chapel schools. And whether the boys acted in public, or in school, as part of their normal training, they could still put to use what they had learned of pronouncing in practice, in addition to what they had been taught theoretically about the figures of rhetoric and the ways in which these had been used by playwrights. The annotations to the text of Palsgraves's *Acolastus* (1540), a play on the theme of the Prodigal Son, are typical of the methods of an Elizabethan teacher taking a dramatic or a non-dramatic work. The pupil's attention is called to the figures in the text, so that when he came to pronounce it he would be able to give what is called a 'figurated pronunciation', that is, he would act it so that the dramatist's organization of language could make an unimpeded impact on the audience.[1]

It was because drama demanded from the person acting the part of a character in a play the same skill in pronouncing as when he was making a speech or preaching a sermon that boys and young men were encouraged to act. And for that reason, too, one Elizabethan writer, Thomas Wright, advised people anxious to improve their pronouncing to go and watch the stage-players, for 'in the substance of external action for most part orators and stage-players agree'. Indeed, Thomas Heywood, the dramatist, was on firm ground when he argued in his *Apology for Actors* (1612) that plays were performed in schools and universities for their educational value, especially in their contribution to the mastery of pronouncing:

To come to Rhetoric it not only emboldens a scholar to speak, but instructs him to speak well, and with judgment

[1] Ed. Carver (1937), p. 145.

to observe his comma's, colons, & full points, his parentheses, his breathing spaces, and distinctions . . . It instructs him to fit his phrases to his action and his action to his phrase, and his pronunciation to them both.

Heywood was stating another educational commonplace when he said that however excellently a speaker might be able to construct a speech, however good the style of his speech itself and the sound of his voice, 'yet without a comely and elegant gesture, a gracious and bewitching kind of action, a natural and familiar motion of the head, the hand, the body, and a moderate and fit countenance, suitable to all the rest, I hold all the rest as nothing'.[1]

There is no need to seek far for the reason for all the attention which was given to the pronouncing of words with 'apt ordering, both of the voice, countenance and all the whole body': it was the belief of the educationalists of the sixteenth century that the exact quality of what is in a speaker's mind needs to be clothed in language which expresses it to perfection; and furthermore, that if an audience is to be affected by perceiving exactly what it is that he is expressing, he must make use of his voice and gesture to ensure that everything that is in his language shall be communicated. What held good of the words of an orator expressing his own thoughts and emotions was believed to apply equally when the speaker was speaking somebody else's words already written or printed: it was the speaker's task to master completely the text which he had to speak, and then, once he had made it his, to use voice and gesture so that the listeners missed nothing of it.

The Elizabethans were taught how to read a text with full understanding of its qualities as literature before they pronounced it: they were also taught to pronounce it so that their understanding of it was communicated to the listeners. And it cannot be emphasized too much that when a text

[1] Sigs. C 3^v–C 4^r.

involved imaginative characterization, the schoolmasters insisted that it ought to be spoken in character. If we learn from the Elizabethans we can find our solution to one of the greatest problems of acting Elizabethan plays: that is, to do full justice to the formal qualities of the lines as literature in such a way that characterization is not impaired but actually improved. At the moment, the formal qualities of the poet's organization of language present a formidable obstacle to the modern actor; but there is no reason why these qualities should not be converted into one of his greatest helps.

When an actor attempts to create character without taking into account the formal qualities of his lines, or when he deliberately comes into conflict with them in his desire to speak with a natural intonation and familiarly realistic manner, he will find it difficult if not impossible to penetrate into the depths of the personage whom the author has imagined. For instance by taking advantage of Shakespeare's 'surcease—success', we find a short way into comprehending and feeling Macbeth's utter lack of pity for Duncan at that moment; the peculiar brand of humour expresses the selfishness of his concern with nothing but himself, and how little he thinks of the deed of murdering the King as such, could he only be sure of success: there is a malevolent complacency in the way in which he contemplates Duncan's 'surcease' being turned into his murderer's 'success'. Similarly, once the actor has made use of the formal pattern of the repetition of 'mock' to realize the objective which Henry V has expressed in it, he will find that he has to emphasize the word each time in order to express what he himself wants in the person of the King: he wants to take the mock that has been directed at him and convert it into something far more harmful, much more deadly, which will go back in its place; he substitutes for it his own brand of gibe, not an empty one, but one which involves a threat to show in practice how mistaken the French have been in their assessing of him, how mistaken

18

the whole world has been in taking his apparently misspent youth at its surface value. Each time the word is used Henry is thinking of his satisfaction in wiping out the insult, in justifying himself, in asserting his true quality, with an awareness of the misery which it will cause, and even a tinge of pity for those who are going to be caught up in the consequences of the ill-starred insult. The actor who has used the pattern of words to identify himself with Henry will necessarily find for himself the right way to emphasize each occurrence of the word 'mock', simply because it is necessary to him for the communicating of what he as Henry wants to say. And the words 'cause to curse' express for Henry a feeling similar to that which lies in 'surcease—success' for Macbeth: again there is a grim humour, a delighted contemplation of a state of affairs which may be too bad for somebody else but will be quite advantageous to the speaker.

To sum up, to deal satisfactorily with Shakespeare we have to remember that while any particular passage is necessarily to be imagined as the speech of a particular character, that character's thought and emotion has been expressed in a skilled organization of language which is rarely, if ever, to be found in the speech of real persons off the stage. If we are to do justice to the skilled organization and still speak the words so that they sound like the unpremeditated speech of a real human being without losing the heightening of art, the first stage of our preparation is to learn from the Elizabethans how to read the text. Then we shall be able to see the way in which the organization of language is also the expression of the wishes of the imagined character: when we can read the play in a modern equivalent of the Elizabethan method we shall find it much easier to embody the character.

Two

READING THE SCORE

THE ELIZABETHAN reading over to himself the following lines of Sidney's sonnet was aware of the way in which thought and emotion had been composed into the pattern of words printed in italics:

Loving in truth, and fain in verse my love to show,
That the dear she might take some *pleasure* of my *pain*,
Pleasure might cause her *read, reading* might make her *know*,
Knowledge might *pity* win, and *pity grace* obtain.

When it came to speaking these lines aloud he inflected his voice and distributed his emphasis in such a way that the listener could respond to the same pattern of thinking and feeling embodied in sound. And it is to speaking on this principle that Fraunce is referring when he tells us: 'By that kind of voice which belongeth to whole sentences, all kinds of figures and passionate ornaments of speech are made manifest.' We cannot hope to know today exactly what 'that kind of voice' was, much less claim to be able to reproduce it; but there is no reason why we should not respond to the figures just as easily as the Elizabethans, and then find our own way of making them 'manifest'.

Using his voice so that the ears and mind of the listener could respond to the words indicated, the Elizabethan led his audience through the pattern in which the poet progresses from an avowal of pain to his assertion of his hope of obtaining the grace which will assuage it: and in doing this the speaker made 'manifest' one of the most effective of the figures in the passage—the figure of *climax*.

Among his examples to illustrate his definition of this figure of *climax* Fraunce actually quotes this first quatrain from Sidney's sonnet: the figure itself he defines as 'a reduplication continued by diverse degrees and steps, as it were, of the same word or sound'.[1] And had he been writing some years later he might well have chosen instead of Sidney's non-dramatic verse the following passage of Shakespeare's dramatic prose:

> For your brother and my sister no sooner *met* but they *look'd*; no sooner *look'd* but they *lov'd*; no sooner *lov'd* but they *sigh'd*; no sooner *sigh'd* but they ask'd one another *the reason*; no sooner knew *the reason* but they sought *the remedy*—and in these degrees have they made a pair of stairs to marriage, which they will climb incontinent, or else be incontinent before marriage.
> (AS YOU LIKE IT, V, ii, 30–36)

Puttenham is thinking along the same lines when he likens this figure to a ladder: he says it 'may be called the marching figure, for after the first step all the rest proceed by double the space, and so in our speech one word proceeds double to the first that was spoken'. And he gives this example:

> His *virtue* made him *wise*, his *wisdom* brought him
> *wealth*,
> His *wealth* won many *friends*, his *friends* made much
> *supply*.

Puttenham says that 'it may as well be called the *climbing* figure, for *Climax* is as much to say as a ladder', particularly in this example, which shows 'how a very mean man

[1] pp. 38 f.

21

by his wisdom and good fortune came to a great estate and dignity'.[1]

In such passages, whatever the Elizabethan actually did with his voice, the result was that the figures were 'made manifest' by the intonation and stress which showed the relation in which the words stand to one another both as sound and as sense. In the foregoing examples and in those which follow in this chapter, italics are used to distinguish the important words in whose arrangement and relation to one another the various figures function. These italics must not be regarded as an attempt to suggest the kind of emphasis which the individual words should be given. The problem of emphasis must be reserved for a later stage of this exposition; it cannot be considered with profit until we have adjusted our minds to reading Shakespeare in a more Elizabethan way, so that we notice, almost as second nature, how he has arranged his words in patterns and relationships. Perhaps it is misleading even to say that he has arranged his words; for that implies a conscious attempt by the dramatist to achieve a certain pattern. Whereas the truth seems to be rather that he had been brought up in a living tradition in which it had become second nature for him to express himself by means of figures; they were not his aim, but expression through them was. The figures are present in his writing, that is indisputable. And in his own day they were not ignored by his actors. Yet, like him, the actors did not see the figures as aims in themselves; an actor did not try to make an antithesis 'manifest' as an aim in itself; he aimed at feeling the emotions and wanting the objectives so that he could seem to be the character; and when he did this for a character whose emotion and objective were expressed in the figure, antithesis, this figure would affect his audience when he was acting. The aim for us today is, therefore, to learn to distinguish almost subconsciously the words which are essential to the functioning of the individual

[1] pp. 207 f.

figures. Again this is not an end in itself. And the actor who can do this will not as a result aim at making his audience hear figures. He will use them in preparation to perceive the emotions and objectives which are expressed in them; he will learn how to express these through them in his acting.

To learn to read Shakespeare in this way is not so difficult a task as it might appear at first sight: the Elizabethans could recognize the words which matter in a figure without anything more advanced in the way of training than the elementary knowledge of the subject available to boys at the grammar schools. But we do not need even as much as that: Elizabethan schoolboys were expected to know all the figures by name, to define them and to identify them where they occurred in a text. But we need only understand the way a figure functions, we have no need to define it or recognize it by name. Thus, once attention has been directed to the kind of pattern with which we have been dealing, no specialized skill or training is required to notice the repetitions in Gertrude's desperate assurance to her son:

> if *words* be made of *breath*
> And *breath* of *life*, I have no *life* to breathe
> What thou hast said to me.

> (HAMLET, III, iv, 197–9)

It is by means of this same 'marching' or 'climbing' figure, this stair of degrees, that Claudius announces the splendour of the ceremonial to accompany Hamlet's duel of honour with Laertes:

> And let the *kettle* to the *trumpet* speak,
> The *trumpet* to the *cannoneer* without,
> The *cannons* to the *heavens*, the *heaven* to the *earth*,
> 'Now the King drinks to Hamlet.'

> (v, ii, 267–70)

23

In *Richard II*, the dethroned King insists in this same pattern:

> The *love* of wicked men converts to *fear*;
> That *fear* to *hate*, and *hate* turns one or both
> To *worthy danger* and *deserved death*.

(v, i, 66–68)

We meet climax again in Troilus's bewilderment:

> If *beauty* have a *soul*, this is not she;
> If *souls* guide *vows*, if *vows* be *sanctimonies*,
> If *sanctimony* be the *gods' delight*,
> If there be rule in unity itself,
> This was not she.

(TROILUS AND CRESSIDA, v, ii, 136–40)

And the same play has another good example in the prose of the comment by Paris on Pandarus's song:

> He eats nothing but doves, love; and *that* breeds *hot blood*, and *hot blood* begets *hot thoughts*, and *hot thoughts* beget *hot deeds*, and *hot deeds* is *love*.

(III, i, 122–4)

Once we have accustomed ourselves to responding to the way in which the words are arranged in such passages as these, we find ourselves noticing the structure of the passage in which Polixenes considers the peril in which he lies:

> This jealousy
> Is for a *precious* creature; as she's *rare*,
> Must it be *great*; and as his person's *mighty*,
> Must it be *violent*; and as he does conceive
> He is dishonour'd by a man which ever
> Profess'd to him, why, his revenges must
> In that be made *more bitter*.

(THE WINTER'S TALE, I, ii, 451–7)

24

Here the thought progresses in a ladder as with climax; but instead of repeating each of his important words to repeat the thought, Shakespeare has substituted a synonym: thus, the idea of 'precious' is repeated in 'rare'; for 'great' he substitutes 'mighty'; and instead of repeating the word 'violence' as another rung in the ladder, he has used one whole line and two half-lines to express the quality of the violence itself in an analysis of its motive: the topmost rung is then reached in the word 'bitter'.

In the following lines Grimald has a slightly different pattern of repetition:

> Come *gentle death*, the *ebb of care*,
> The *ebb of care*, the *flood of life*,
> The *flood of life*, the *joyful fare*,
> The *joyful fare*, etc.

Here there is as before a repetition of the last word or words of one statement in the next, but there is no mounting progress of thought: it is in this respect that this pattern differs from climax. Where climax is progressive, this figure, called *Anadiplosis*, is static. It is used by Shakespeare in Hamlet's outburst of revulsion:

> Eyes without *feeling, feeling* without sight.
>
> (III, iv, 78)

Shakespeare and his contemporaries often use patterns of sound such as these. Spenser, who makes great and effective use of them, gives us one example in this alexandrine from *The Faery Queene*: here equivalent ideas involve the repetition of almost the same words, but in an inverted order.

> Which *still wex old* in *wo*, while *wo still wexeth new*.
>
> (I, ix, 9)

The Duke's irony depends upon a manipulation of words in this way in his retort to Orlando:

What would you have? Your *gentleness* shall *force*
More than your *force* move us to *gentleness*.

(AS YOU LIKE IT, II, vii, 102–3)

It should be noted that the effect is also due to some extent to the fact that 'force' is used first as a verb and then as a noun. There is the same figure of reversal with its interchange of words in Leontes' assurance:

who mayst see,
Plainly as *heaven sees earth* and *earth sees heaven*.

(THE WINTER'S TALE, I, ii, 314–15)

Once we have come to notice how the order of the words which are repeated has been changed in passages such as these, we have in fact responded to the functioning of the figure called Anti-metabole, whether we know or do not know that such a figure exists, what it is called and how it may be defined. It is a figure, says Puttenham, which 'takes a couple of words to play with in a verse, and by making them to change and shift one into other's place, they do very prettily exchange and shift the sense'.[1] But it is not essential to know that to be able to recognize how Shakespeare has constructed the line in which Lucius tells the disguised Imogen:

Thy name well fits *thy faith, thy faith thy name*.

(CYMBELINE, IV, ii, 384)

Shakespeare has often written passages in which the same words or sounds occur at the end as at the beginning: for example, there is the abrupt summing-up by Coriolanus, when he denounces the interference of the populace in the processes of government:

Purpose so barr'd, it follows
Nothing is done to *purpose*.

(III, i, 148–9)

[1] pp. 208 f.

26

In *King John* when the Citizen on the walls refuses to accept either the French or the English claim to Angiers until one has prevailed over the other, he declares:

> *Blood* hath bought *blood*, and *blows* have answer'd *blows*;
> *Strength* match'd with *strength*, and *power* confronted *power*;
>
> (II, i, 329–30)

And Paris adds rhyme to another example of this pattern in the rounded conclusion to his plea for Helen not to be delivered up to the Greeks:

> Then, I say,
> *Well* may we fight for her whom we know *well*
> The world's large spaces cannot parallel.
>
> (TROILUS AND CRESSIDA, II, ii, 160–2)

In a prose passage Sidney writes:

> *The thoughts* are but overflowings of the mind, and the tongue is but a servant of *the thoughts*.

Like other Elizabethans, he knew that he was using the figure named Epanalepsis: and Fraunce quotes this particular passage as an example of the figure, together with some lines of Sidney's verse:

> *Fear* is more pain, than is the pain it *fears*.
> *They love* indeed, who quake to say *they love*.
> *Hark* plaintful ghosts, infernal furies *hark*.

Fraunce's definition of this figure is what we would expect from the way in which we have seen it functioning in practice: it occurs, he says, 'when the same sound is iterated in the beginning and ending'.[1] Puttenham calls epanalepsis 'the echo sound', adding, 'Unless I called him

[1] p. 45.

27

the *echo sound*, I could not tell what name to give him, unless it were the slow return'.[1] But the echo comes back with a certain crispness in the retort:

Cassius from bondage will deliver *Cassius*.

(JULIUS CAESAR, I, iii, 90)

The Elizabethan who noticed what Puttenham calls the 'change and shift one into other's place' of *name* and *faith* in the line from *Cymbeline* which has already been quoted would not have failed to observe that 'the same sound is iterated in the beginning and ending':

Thy name well fits thy faith, thy faith *thy name*.

Nor would the repetition in the middle of the line have gone unnoticed:

Thy name well fits *thy faith, thy faith* thy name.

(IV, ii, 384)

There is another example of this sort of repetition in the last line of Sidney's Sonnet XXXIII:

But to *my self, my self* did give the blow.

The pattern is also found in Nestor's declaration:

—why, then the thing of courage,
As rous'd *with rage, with rage* doth sympathize.

(TROILUS AND CRESSIDA, I, iii, 51–52)

The following example from Raleigh is quoted by Puttenham:

With wisdom's eyes had but blind fortune seen,
Then had *my love, my love* for ever been.

And Puttenham's name for this particular pattern is 'the Underlay, or Cuckoo-spell'. The more formal writers on

[1] p. 200.

rhetoric, and the schoolteachers, used the term Epizeuxis. As we see, it can be used as a means to an end, the perfect expression of what the writer can say only by means of it: but like' all the other figures it can also be abused, and the modern suspicion of repetitions of sound seems justified by another example given by Puttenham:

> The chiefest staff of mine assured stay,
> With no small grief *is gone, is gone* away.[1]

It might be argued that the repetition intensifies the grief here, yet it is difficult not to feel that the poet was more concerned with the decorative sound than with the meaning, and that he was glad to find two more syllables so easily to fill up the second line of his couplet. But in the other examples which have been given, sound aids sense, intensifying emotion, especially in the chagrin of Sidney's admission that he himself was responsible for his pain.

The Elizabethans sometimes use patterns of words having almost but not quite the same sound, and then the juxtaposition helps to focus attention on the play of meaning as well as adding music to the line. Henry V's 'cause to curse', and Macbeth's 'surcease, success' are examples of this figure, as we have already noticed. It is also present in Romeo's remorseful:

> what says
> My *conceal'd* lady to our *cancell'd* love?

> (ROMEO AND JULIET, III, iii, 97–98)

In the Duchess of York's play on words there is a genuine bitterness:

> Ah, that deceit should steal such gentle shape,
> And with a virtuous *vizor* hide deep *vice*.

> (RICHARD III, II, ii, 27–28)

[1] p. 201.

And again, bitterness surges through the same figure in Troilus' disillusioned apostrophe to Cressida:

> Let all untruths *stand* by thy *stained* name,
> And they'll seem glorious.
> (TROILUS AND CRESSIDA, V, ii, 177–8)

The bitterness is one of shame in the assertion made by Cassius:

> I had as *lief* not be as *live* to be
> In awe of such a thing as I myself.
> (JULIUS CAESAR, I, ii, 94–95)

Possibly the most ingeniously witty retort in the whole of Shakespeare is Hamlet's sneer:

> A little more than *kin*, and less than *kind*.

This is an example of the figure, Paronomasia, which is defined by Fraunce as occurring 'when a word is changed in signification by changing a letter or syllable'[1]. He quotes as an example Sidney's lines:

> Those lamps of heavenly fire to fixed motion bound,
> The *ever* turning spheres, the *never* moving ground.

Sidney is also quoted by Puttenham: 'Sir Philip Sidney in a ditty played very prettily with these two words, *love* and *live*, thus.

> And all my life I will confess,
> The less I *love*, I *live* the less.'

Shakespeare has numerous examples of this figure, among them the abrupt retort of Troilus:

> Let Paris bleed: 'tis but a *scar* to *scorn*;
> (I, i, 110)

Prosonomasia lends itself particularly to irony and wit. There is Volumnia's cynically realistic:

[1]pp. 49 f.

Thy knee *bussing* the stones—for in such *business*
Action is eloquence.

(CORIOLANUS, III, ii, 75–76)

When Iago uses the figure his malice blazes triumphantly:

But, O, what damned minutes tells he o'er
Who *dotes*, yet *doubts*, suspects, yet strongly loves!

(OTHELLO, III, iii, 173–4)

Puttenham refers to the figure as Prosonomasia as well as Paronomasia, and as usual, he has his own English name for it—'the Nicknamer'. He says it is 'a figure by which ye play with a couple of words or names much resembling, and because the one seems to answer th' other by manner of allusion, and doth, as it were, nick him, I call him the *Nicknamer*'. Among the examples which he gives are figures which are almost reproduced in essence in some of Shakespeare's work. For instance, in *Troilus and Cressida*, Nestor declares:

In the *reproof* of chance
Lies the *true proof* of men.

(I, iii, 33–34)

And Puttenham's example runs:

Prove me madame ere ye fall to *reprove*,
Meek minds should rather *excuse* than *accuse*.[1]

Here the second line has the same play upon 'excuse—accuse' as occurs in the well-known passage of dialogue between Richard and Anne in *Richard III*. He pleads for leisure 'to excuse myself', but she answers that the only 'excuse current' that he can make is to hang himself: to this he retorts:

By such despair I should accuse myself.

(I, ii, 82–85)

[1] pp. 202 f.

For us today the play upon 'surcease—success' in Macbeth's soliloquy is an example of paronomasia, as we have already noted. But in Shakespeare's day the two words were almost perfect rhymes. As a result, to Elizabethans they probably sounded more like repetitions of the same sound than a play upon slightly different sounds. Repetition of the same sound, but with a different meaning each time, was what we found in Henry V's use of the word 'mock'. There is the same kind of echo in Spenser's famous sonnet:

> *Vain* man, said she, that dost in *vain* assay.
> (AMORETTI, LXXXV)

This figure allows the King to put extra venom into his dismissal of Northumberland at the beginning of *Henry IV*, Part I:

> You have good *leave* to *leave* us.
> (I, iii, 20)

And the play on words adds insult to the threat of injury in Duke Frederick's command to Oliver:

> Bring him dead or *living*
> Within this twelvemonth, or turn thou no more
> To seek a *living* in our territory.
> (AS YOU LIKE IT, III, i, 6–8)

Changes in pronunciation have almost destroyed for us Shakespeare's emphasis on the paradox of evil's seeming fairness in Banquo's words to Macbeth. As 'ea' and 'ai' were pronounced almost as homonyms, there was more bite in the question:

> Good sir, why do you start, and seem to *fear*
> Things that do sound so *fair*?
> (MACBETH, I, iii, 51–52)

Whenever we find a pun in Shakespeare we are perfectly entitled to give it the more imposing title of *Antanaclasis*:

but whatever we call it, and even if we give it no name at all, we can still respond to its functioning merely by being aware of the pattern of sound which calls attention to a play upon meaning. Sidney's example is obvious enough, for instance:

My forces *raz'd*, thy banners *rais'd* within.

One of the felicities of Shakespeare's Sonnet No. 18 is to be found in the last line:

So long *lives* this, and this *gives* *l*ife to thee.

The sound 'ives' of 'lives' is repeated in the word 'gives', and the first letter, 'l', is repeated in 'life'. And the compression of meaning in this statement comes in addition from the fact that 'lives' and 'life' derive from the same etymological root: a further point to notice is that these two words were much more alike in sound in Shakespeare's day. The same kind of play on sound and meaning occurs twice in Troilus' lines:

But alas,
I am as *true* as *truth's simplicity*,
And *simpler* than the infancy of *truth*.
(TROILUS AND CRESSIDA, III, ii, 164–6)

We find it again in Prospero's rueful:

new *created*
The *creatures* that were mine.
(THE TEMPEST, I, ii, 81–82)

And it is in the rapture of Ferdinand's:

Admir'd Miranda!
Indeed the top of *admiration*.
(III, i, 37–38)

This figure is another example of what are known as figures of words. In the rhetoric books it is called *Polyptoton*, and is defined by Fraunce as 'often falling or declining of one word'. He gives an English example from Sidney:

Thou art of *blood*, joy not to make things *bleed*:
Thou fearest *death*, think they are loth to *die*.[1]

The play upon 'life' and 'live' which we find in the last line of Shakespeare's sonnet also occurs in one of the examples which Puttenham gives of polyptoton:

Who *lives* in love his *life* is full of fears

And in this case there is also a repetition of slightly different sounds in 'lives' and 'love'. Puttenham gives the figure its Latin name, *Traductio*, but adds his own, 'the tranlacer'. It occurs when 'ye turn and tranlace a word into many sundry shapes as the tailor doth his garment'. The 'tranlacing' continues throughout four lines of his first example:

Who *lives* in love his *life* is full of fears,
To lose his love, his *livelode* or liberty
But *lively* sprights that young and reckless be,
Think that there is no *living* like to theirs.

He tells us that we see how 'this word life is tranlaced into live, living, lively, livelode'.[2]

Ullysses tranlaces in his praise of Troilus:

Speaking in *deeds* and *deedless* in his tongue.

(TROILUS AND CRESSIDA, IV, v, 98)

The figure occurs again in Nestor's chivalrous declaration to Hector:

I would my arms could match thee in *contention*
As they *contend* with thee in courtesy.

(IV, v, 205–6)

[1] pp. 51 f.
[2] pp. 203 f.

It is by means of polyptoton that Proteus considers how love bade him 'swear' and now bids him 'forswear', before he exclaims in the very same figure:

> *Unheedful* vows may *heedfully* be broken.
> (THE TWO GENTLEMEN OF VERONA, II, vi, 11)

Polyptoton lends itself particularly well to the type of arguing known technically as arguing from cognates: it is the way in which Antony reasons over Caesar's body:

> If it were so, it was a *grievous* fault;
> And *grievously* hath Caesar answer'd it.
> (JULIUS CAESAR, III, ii, 79–80)

Enobarbus uses the same method to persuade himself that he has every reason to desert Antony:

> The loyalty well held to *fools* does make
> Our faith mere *folly*.
> (ANTONY AND CLEOPATRA, III, xiii, 42–43)

We have already considered how much of the effect of Hamlet's, 'A little more than kin, and less than kind' depends upon the extension of 'kin' into 'kind'; but another pattern which is almost as important is the linking together of 'more' and 'less'. There is something similar in the lines in which Theseus in *A Midsummer Night's Dream* declares with the true condescension of the great of soul:

> Love, therefore, and tongue-tied simplicity
> In *least* speak *most* to my capacity.
> (V, I, 104–5)

In each case contrasting ideas are joined together to make an expressive and compressed statement. The arranging of words in this kind of pattern of equivalence or of opposition makes it possible for the playwright to ensure that the individual ideas can be distinguishable within comparatively complex, and yet succinct, statements. In the following passage, for instance, Gratiano has three words in the first line, each of which has an equivalent in the second; and in this case, each of the equivalents expresses the contrary idea to that expressed by the first line respectively:

> And let my *liver* (1) rather *heat* (2) with *wine* (3)
> Than my *heart* (1) *cool* (2) with mortifying *groans* (3).
> (THE MERCHANT OF VENICE, I, i, 81–2)

There are actually four pairs of ideas, involving four sets of words, in the complaint by Troilus:

> Why should *I* (1) *war* (2) *without* (3) *the walls of Troy* (4)
> *That* (1) *find such cruel battle* (2) *here* (4) *within* (3)?
> (TROILUS AND CRESSIDA, I, i 2–3)

The sets are as follows: (1) I—that; (2) war—find such cruel battle; (3) without—within; (4) the walls of Troy—here.

To conjoin contrasting ideas in this way is to use what the rhetoricians called the figure of *Antithesis*. Puttenham gives a straightforward example which is not so rich in added meaning as those from Shakespeare just quoted:

> *Good* have I done you, much, *harm* did I never none,
> Ready to *joy* your *gaines*, your *losses* to *bemoan*,
> Why therefore should you *grudge* so sore at *my welfare*:
> Who *only bred your bliss*, and *never caused your care*.[1]

Leontes' declaration of remorse and joy has six sets of ideas in what is a complicated and yet precise statement:

[1] p. 210.

> Which had been done
> But that the *good mind* (1) *of Camillo* (2) *tardied* (3)
> *My* (2) *swift* (3) *command*, (1) though I with *death* (4) and with
> *Reward* (4) did *threaten* (5) and *encourage* (5) him,
> *Not doing it* (6) and *being done*. (6)
>
> (THE WINTER'S TALE, III, ii, 158–62)

The equivalents are as follows: (1) good mind—command; (2) of Camillo—my; (3) tardied—swift; (4) with death—with reward; (5) threaten—encourage; (6) not doing it—being done.

The first two sets should not be regarded as merely mechanical or phonological: Leontes is re-experiencing the horror of his swift command, imagining once again just how ruthless, treacherous and vile was the jealous rage surging through him; gratefully, as one who has been saved from the worst through another's virtue, he delights in the thought of Camillo's 'good mind': all this is expressed partly in the antithesis of 'command' and 'good mind', and partly in that of 'my' and 'of Camillo'. In each case the verbal pattern expresses a fundamental contrast of idea and of emotion.

The speech with which Ferdinand opens the third act of *The Tempest* has as many as eleven sets of contrasting ideas:

> There be some *sports* (1) are *painful*, (1) and *their labour* (2)
> *Delight in them* (2) sets off; some kinds of *baseness* (3)
> Are *nobly* (3) undergone, and most *poor* (4) *matters* (5)
> Point to *rich* (4) *ends* (5). This my mean task
> Would be as *heavy* (6) to me as *odious*, (6) but
> *The mistress* (7) which I serve *quickens* (8) *what* (7)*'s dead* (8)
> And makes my *labours* (9) *pleasures*. (9) O, *she is* (10)
> *Ten times more gentle* (11) than her *father's* (10) *crabbed* (11)
> And he's composed of harshness.   (III, i, 1–9)

Ferdinand has expressed the paradox perfectly in conjoining the following pairs of contrasting ideas: (1) sports—painful; (2) their labour—delight in them; (3) baseness—nobly; (4) poor—rich; (5) matters—ends; (6) heavy—odious; (7) the mistress—what; (8) quickens—'s dead; (9) labours—pleasures; (10) she is—father's; (11) ten times more gentle—crabbed. The sixth set as shown here is not actually of contrasting ideas, but there is a contrast between the fact that the labours are not as heavy as they are odious expressed in the line 'Would be as heavy to me as odious', in which there is an implied antithesis between 'would be' and an understood 'it is' or ''tis'.

To reason in this way by means of contraries stimulates attention in virtue of the seeming incompatibility of the terms which are joined together; this is Pisanio's reasoning in *Cymbeline*:

> Wherein I am *false* I am *honest*: *not true* to *be true*.
>
> (IV, iii, 42)

Puttenham's name for this figure is the 'Cross-couple', which others call Synoeciosis. He gives as an example:

> The covetous miser of all his goods ill got,
> As well wants *what he hath*, as *that he hath not*.[1]

The figure combines the emotions in Hamlet's, 'I must be *cruel* only to be *kind*.' (III, iv, 178.) The 'cross-couple' is involved also in Adam's bitter outburst in *As You Like It*:

> Your *virtues*, gentle master,
> Are *sanctified and holy traitors* to you.
> O, what a world is this, when *what is comely*
> *Envenoms* him that bears it!   (II, iii, 12–15)

And Claudio, intellectually, if not emotionally, convinced by the Duke, declares:

[1]pp. 206 f.

> *To sue to live,* I *find* I *seek to die;*
> And *seeking death, find life.*
>
> (MEASURE FOR MEASURE, III, i, 42–43)

Earlier, before the Duke's speech, Claudio's words come in the form of antithesis:

> I *have hope* (1) *to live,* (2) and *am prepar'd* (1) *to die* (2)
>
> (III, i, 4)

There is an even closer joining of contradictory ideas in Juliet's anguished denunciation of her husband when she hears of Tybalt's death:

> Beautiful tyrant! fiend angelical!
> Dove-feather'd raven! wolfish-ravening lamb!

This is the figure Oxymoron, used again three lines later:

> A damned saint, an honourable villain!
>
> (ROMEO AND JULIET, III, ii, 75–76; 79)

All the figures which have been discussed so far in this chapter belong to the category of figures of words; and it is to these that Fraunce refers when he talks of 'sweet repetitions and dimensions'.[1] A figure of words is in essence a pattern of sound; the pattern need not be used to enforce the sense, but in most cases, especially with Shakespeare, meaning and emotion are bound up in the structure of the pattern. We are accustomed to estimating a writer's skill with three figures of words—rhyme, alliteration and assonance—in accordance with his power of using the sound pattern as a structural element of expression rather than as a decoration only. To learn how to read Shakespeare's score before attempting to speak it, we have merely to become as responsive to all the figures of words as we are already to rhyme, alliteration and assonance. Once this step has been taken we are in a position to find a way of speaking the lines

[1] p. 207.

as they should be spoken so that the audience can respond to the poet's art.

We have seen that it does not matter whether we can identify any particular pattern by the name under which it is to be found in the textbooks of renaissance Rhetoric: what matters is that the reader's mind should become accustomed to recognizing the way in which the poet has organized language in a relationship between words as sounds which is also a relationship of thought and emotion. Consider, for instance, Caesar's lines:

> Sister, prove such a wife
> As my thoughts make thee, and as my farthest band
> Shall pass on thy approof.

(ANTONY AND CLEOPATRA, III, ii, 25–27)

It is enough for us to understand the organization of the words, so that we see how the meaning has been composed in the arrangement in which 'prove' has as its equivalents 'make' and 'pass', while 'Sister', or the understood 'you', has the counterparts 'my thoughts' and 'my farthest band'. Similarly, with 'prove' and 'approof', without being able to define Polyptoton, and in utter ignorance of the existence of any such name, it is enough for a reader to respond to the relationship between the words; indeed, it is far better for him to react to this relationship in fact than for him merely to be able to recognize and name the figure in an empty and mechanical way.[1]

Whether they are monologue or dialogue, verse or prose, Shakespeare's speeches become at once richer and simpler when the score is read in the way that is advocated here.

---

[1]It has been suggested to me by Mr. Duncan Ross, Principal of the Bristol Old Vic Theatre School, that some people may find it easier, in fact, to recognize figures by learning their names and definitions. Such people would be well advised to make the extra effort, but nobody should be deterred from reacting to Shakespeare's art by an inability to digest lists of Greek and Latin names, or even English definitions.

His complexity ceases to be obscurely complicated, his meaning becomes deeper and yet more accessible. In a passage such as the following in the prose of Benedick's soliloquy a reader quite ignorant of the names or definitions of the figures involved can proceed from a full awareness of structure to a more complete understanding of the meaning:

> One woman is fair, yet I am well; another is wise, yet
> I am well; another is virtuous, yet I am well; but till
> all graces be in one woman, one woman shall not come
> into my grace.
> (MUCH ADO, II, iii)

In the pattern, the first word 'one' is matched by 'another' and 'another'; 'fair' is matched by 'wise' and 'virtuous'; and 'yet I am well' is repeated three times. The final statement is rich in tightly compressed meaning, but, thanks to its structural organization, is particularly lucid: 'all' has its counterparts in 'one' and 'one'; 'be' is matched with 'shall not come', and 'in one woman' with 'into my grace'. Here, too, are the same three figures as we found in the line from *Cymbeline* ('Thy name well fits thy faith, thy faith thy name'). The statement begins and ends with 'grace' (in two separate meanings); in the middle there is repetition of 'one woman'; and the order of 'all graces be in one woman' has been reversed in 'one woman shall not come into my grace'.

In *A Midsummer Night's Dream*, when Theseus chuckles 'Our sport shall be to *take* what they *mistake*' (v, i, 90), it does not matter if we do not know that here is an example of prosonomasia, so long as we notice the play on 'take— mistake', together with the fact that 'our sport' has a structural equivalent in 'they'.

And complete ignorance of the name and definition of the figure Zeugma (in which one verb is used to supply several congruent clauses) does not prevent an alert mind from responding to the patterning of Pisanio's words:

41

> But for my mistress,
> I nothing know where she remains, why gone,
> Nor when she purposes to return.
>
> (CYMBELINE, IV, iii, 13–15)

In these lines one set of equivalents consists of 'where', 'why', 'when'; another runs, 'remains', 'gone', 'purposes to return'; and the mind reacts also to the repetition, and implied repetition of 'she' in each clause.

When we have become attuned to the way in which Shakespeare and his contemporaries wrote we find ourselves noticing over and over again the presence of sets of equivalents, of balancings and repetitions in his work. The venom of Regan's pitiless sneer is expressed in an arrangement of words resembling the pattern of antithesis:

> I pray you, father, *being* weak, *seem* so.
>
> (KING LEAR, II, iv, 200)

The underlying insistence is upon the difference between reality and appearance; Regan strips her father of illusion, exposes him to derision, by expressing through this compact arrangement a curt command not to try to appear what he is not. There is a similar structure in Lear's statement earlier:

> Meantime we shall *express* our *darker* purpose.
>
> (I, i, 35)

And here a contrast is implied between 'express' (in the sense of bringing out into the light) and 'darker'.

Much of the force of Kent's reply to Lear comes from the compression of his thought and emotion into sets of equivalents:

> Be Kent unmannerly
> When Lear is mad. What wouldst thou do, old man?
> Think'st thou that duty shall have dread to speak,
> When power to flattery bows. To plainness honour's
>   bound
> When majesty falls to folly.   (I, i, 144–8)

42

The equivalents are as follows: 'be'—'is'; 'Kent'—'Lear'; 'unmannerly'—'mad'; 'duty'—'power'; 'shall have dread' —'bows'; 'to speak'—'to flattery'; 'to plainness'—'to folly'; 'honour'—'majesty'; ' 's bound'—'falls'.

When we do not read the text in the way which is suggested here we run the risk of finding ourselves in the difficulty referred to by Stanislavski. He quotes W. S. Jevons as the authority for saying that in Enobarbus' lines Shakespeare 'had joined in this one phrase six subjects and six predicates, so that strictly speaking we have six times six, or thirty-six prepositions'.

> Hoo! hearts, tongues, figures, scribes, bards, poets, cannot
> Think, speak, cast, write, sing, number,—hoo!—
> His love to Antony.
>
> (ANTONY AND CLEOPATRA, III, ii, 16–18)[1]

Stanislavski despairs, quite rightly, of an actor ever being able to express an awareness of all thirty-six prepositions to an audience. But it is, I think, a mistake to regard the passage as having this complexity. It has six subjects, but each of these has only one predicate and no more: 'hearts'— 'think'; 'tongues'—'speak'; 'figures'—'cast'; 'scribes'— 'write'; 'bards'—'sing'; 'poets'—'number'. The whole force of the passage depends upon the fact that Enobarbus ironically spins out a list of nouns as proof of the allegedly abounding and sincere love of Lepidus for Antony, and then no less ironically provides each noun with a verb to complete the picture of overwhelming activity, all inspired by Lepidus' love.

The Elizabethan reader would not have made the modern mistake. He would have connected each noun with its respective predicate as a matter of course, and would also have recognized the figure by its name, *Brachylogia*.

---

[1]C. Stanislavski, *Building a Character* (1950), pp. 161 f.

Puttenham calls it 'the cutted comma', explaining, 'We use sometimes to proceed all by single words, without any close or coupling, saving that a little pause or comma is given to every word. This figure for pleasure may be called in our vulgar the cutted comma, for that there cannot be a shorter division than at every word's end.'[1] Fraunce puts an example of Brachylogia taken from Sidney among a group of miscellaneous figures at the end of the section which he devotes to figures of words:

> Vertue, (a) beauty (b) and speech, (c) did strike, (a)
>   wound, (b) charm, (c)
> My heart, (a) eyes, (b) ears, (c) with wonders, (a)
>   love, (b) delight. (c)
> First (a), second, (b) last, (c) did bind, (a) enforce (b)
>   and arm, (c)
> His works, (a) shows, (b) suits, (c) with wit, (a) grace
>   (b) and vows' might. (c)[2]

Yet, without knowing the name of the figure, but simply by reading alertly, determined to absorb the meaning which comes in word-relationship, we can recognize the same kind of patterning of words and meaning in the lines of Leontes:

> Though I with death (a) and with
> Reward (b) did threaten (a) and encourage (b) him,
> Not doing (a) it and being done. (b)
>
> (THE WINTER'S TALE, III, ii, 160–2)

It cannot be emphasized too often that there is no need for us today to make ourselves expert in a theoretical and formal art of rhetoric in order to perceive and to understand how a poet of the past has composed his thought and emotion into arrangements of words and sounds according to a theory and practice which was taught formally in his day. On the one hand, we have to recognize that if we

[1] p. 213.
[2] p. 56.

approach a passage of Shakespeare primarily by way of systematic analysis into the individual rhetorical figures, we shall find that it leads to a complete imaginative realizing of his meaning. But, on the other hand, if we approach the same passage utterly resolved to master the meaning as it is expressed in every individual word in its context with all the others, then we shall find ourselves noticing how individual words and ideas stand in relation to one another as combinations and patterns of vowels and consonants. The details of which we are then aware will be the same as we would have come to recognize had we started with the rhetorical analysis.

For instance, when we read carefully the lines in which Macbeth expresses his dissatisfaction with himself before he goes to murder Duncan, we find that ultimately we react in exactly the same way as if we had first analysed them into the structure of the figures and then imagined them in the light of the analysis:

> Whiles I threat, he lives;
> Words to the heat of deeds too cold breath gives.
>
> (MACBETH, II, i, 60–61)

As the actor of Macbeth makes himself grasp the meaning of the first line completely he realizes that the thane is contrasting what he does with what is being done by Duncan, and that he must stop doing what he is doing if he is to make Duncan stop living: then naturally, as a matter of course, 'I' is contrasted with 'he', and 'threat' with 'lives'. And with the understanding that the second line means that words give too cold breath to the heat of deeds thus preventing their being accomplished, again quite naturally 'words' is contrasted with 'deeds', and the idea of 'heat' with that of 'too cold breath'. And an actor would arrive at exactly this point if he started with a rhetorical analysis and then passed on to an imaginative realization of the meaning.

If we concentrate on following the sense of a line scrupulously we will notice not only how the figures of words function as such, but how the author has composed his thoughts in tropes and figures of sentence as well. And here, too, there is no need to know the name of a figure in order to understand how it operates, and to respond to the word or words in virtue of which it functions.

The Elizabethans were taught carefully to recognize 'in what word the Emphasis lyeth, and therefore which is to be elevated in pronunciation. As namely those words in which the chief Trope or Figure is'.[1] Just as we cannot say what was done with the voice in pronouncing figures of words, so there is nothing for us to say about its use in the handling of tropes or figures of sentence. But with all three kinds of arrangements of language we can say that what the author had done was 'made manifest' to the listener. Of tropes, for instance, Fraunce says: 'In the particular applying of the voice to several (i.e. individual) words, we make tropes that be most excellent plainly appear.' And he adds, quite logically, that 'without this change of voice, neither any *Ironia*, nor lively *Metaphor* well be discerned'.[2] Once more the point must be made, of course, that the actor's preparation is not aimed at making the audience conscious of the figures for their own sakes. The techniques, first of reading the figures and recognizing the effective words, and then of inflecting the voice, are both subordinated to creating the character. The actor should not be deterred from preparing in this way, or from making use of the preparation in actual performance, by the thought that his audience cannot possibly notice the individual details of what he is doing. His aim should be the most complete and satisfactory performance of the lines which the character speaks. Even when his audience does not recognize the details of what he is doing, the fact that he has mastered these details and

[1]Brinsley, p. 213.
[2]p. 106.

subordinated them in his portrayal of real emotion and in real striving for an objective will make his performance all the better. His aim is not to affect an audience by a certain technique as an end in itself, but to incorporate the technique into his playing, and affect them by his creation of the role. Edmund Kean was often mistaken for an entirely spontaneous actor who had not worked out his effects carefully. Yet, in fact, he would practise an intonation punctiliously until he was able to reproduce it undeviatingly in performance after performance, just as a singer can reproduce the same note in the same way. And each time the intonation was effective because it was used by the actor to externalize an emotion which he really felt.

The modern task is to recognize the words through which the tropes function; then we can consider how we, today, might 'change', that is inflect, the voice so that the trope may 'well be discerned'.

Figures of words usually involve more than one word in a pattern of sound; but often with tropes one word only is affected. This is particularly true of the trope which is probably mentioned most in modern criticism, metaphor. In Kent's apostrophe to the sun (in itself a figure of sentence) the single word 'beacon' is used metaphorically for 'sun': this is the word in which 'the chief trope is':

> Approach, thou beacon to this under globe.
>
> (KING LEAR, II, ii, 158)

When Edgar describes to his blind father the view which he claims to see from the top of the imagined cliff, we can find the most important word in which the chief trope is merely by concentrating on the meaning:

> The crows and choughs that wing the mid-way air
> Show scarce so gross as beetles.
>
> (IV, vi, 13–14)

47

The word 'wing' in the first line has been used to denote
what is done by means of a wing, that is, flying; and when
we read the line our picture of the birds in motion comes
from giving the word its figurative meaning. The trope in
this case is metonymy; and where the Elizabethans would
have recognized 'wing' as the important word to be
emphasized because they knew its importance to the trope,
we find ourselves reaching the same conclusion simply
because the sense of the line takes us there.

In the next line of Edgar's description two ideas are
linked, 'scarce so gross' and 'as beetles'. The simile comes to
life only if we image in our minds the size of beetles, and
picture birds below us at such a distance that they appear so
diminished. An actor has to speak the simile so that the
audience sees in its mind's eye the birds so far below when
no more than half-way down; nobody can say categorically
how this is to be done, or what it is to sound like in practice;
but on the other hand, we can insist that no actor can do it
unless he understands how the units of composition in which
the author has expressed himself are related to one another.
The simile is a likening of the size of birds to that of beetles;
and the actor's voice must image the relationship which
exists both in the text and in his mind.

Figure of sentence is the third and last kind of rhetorical
figure to be considered; and here, again, the reader who
concentrates on the meaning will automatically react to the
functioning of the figure. If, for instance, we read Kent's
words 'Approach, thou beacon,' realizing that it is addressed
to the sun as if to a sentient being, we will find ourselves
imagining him speaking and thinking the word 'approach'
as if it were an apostrophe, which in fact it is. As such, of
course, it is a figure of sentence. Lady Macbeth's 'Come,
you spirits,' is another figure of sentence; so is her command,
'Give me the daggers.'

What is important for the modern actor of Shakespeare is
to realize that the figures are not there merely for their own

sake; and this is true even of the early Shakespeare. The modern mind is most easily disconcerted by figures of words; and for this reason the point cannot be stressed too firmly or too often that Shakespeare is almost always using them to crystallize something which he is imagining in the person of the character who speaks. To recognize the pattern and to work with it is, as a result, in most cases a help to imagining more fully. The actor finds himself master of the meaning more completely, of a meaning which involves emotion and the implications which deepen and enrich bare sense into something which defies exhaustive paraphrase. For instance, it is through the patterning of Juliet's line and a half that we can penetrate to what is fundamental to Shakespeare's imagining of her character and part in the action:

> And for thy name, which is no part of thee,
> Take all myself.

The more obvious elements of the pattern are the balancing of 'for'—'take' and 'thy name'—'myself'. But there is also the antithesis of 'no part'—'all', by means of which the relationship between 'thy', 'of thee' and 'myself' is made apparent. At the most superficial level this is a conceit involving the play upon 'no part' and 'all' and the distinction between a person's essence and his name: but as we ponder the full meaning of what the patterning outlines, we find a sincere refusal to be deterred by forms and conventions, a genuine resolution to give up everything that being a Montagu has meant to her till now in the ignoring of what Capulet has likewise meant. Juliet's bounty is already as 'boundless as the sea'; she is already bestowing all of herself; within her personality nothing is withheld, she is utterly committed in her love. From now on, as the play is to show, Romeo is all her family, more to her than 'father, mother, cousin, all'. And all this is already involved in the antithesis of 'no part' and 'all'. Already her objective is plain; Romeo is the centre of her life; without him there is to be no life for her; and much as she draws what she needs from him, she sees their relationship already as one in which she will give generously rather than take.

In whole speeches, as well as in smaller passages, it will be found that attention to structure leads to a clarification of the objective. It is well known that Shakespeare has written many speeches which, while they are not set orations, are constructed in accordance with a standard pattern of argument based on enthemyme which was to be learned in the Elizabethan grammar school. Professor T. W. Baldwin and Sister Miriam Joseph have pointed out, for instance, that when the Duke exhorts Claudio to prepare himself for death in *Measure for Measure*, his first insistence is the equivalent of the proposition with which an argument might be begun in an exercise of formal logic:[1]

> Be absolute for death; either death or life
> Shall thereby be the sweeter.

This 'proposition' is now supported by what is known as the minor premise:

> Reason thus with life.
> If I do lose thee, I do lose a thing
> That none but fools would keep.

And the minor premise is proved by the eleven subsequent arguments:

> (1)   A breath thou art,
> Servile to all the skyey influences,
> That dost this habitation where thou keep'st
> Hourly afflict.
> (2)   Merely thou art Death's fool;
> For him thou labour'st by thy flight to shun
> And yet run'st towards him still
> (3)   Thou art not noble;

---

[1]Baldwin, *op. cit.*, II, 84 f; Sister M. Joseph, *Shakespeare's Use of the Arts of Language* (1947), pp. 182 f.

For all th' accommodations that thou bear'st
Are nurs'd by baseness.

(4)   Thou 'rt by no means valiant;
For thou dost fear the soft and tender fork
Of a poor worm. Thy best of rest is sleep,
And that thou oft provok'st; yet grossly fear'st
Thy death, which is no more.

(5)   Thou art not thyself;
For thou exists on many a thousand grains
That issue out of dust.

(6)   Happy thou art not;
For what thou hast not, still thou striv'st to get,
And what thou hast, forget'st.

(7)   Thou art not certain;
For thy complexion shifts to strange effects,
After the moon.

(8)   If thou art rich, thou 'rt poor;
For like an ass whose back with ingots bows,
Thou bear'st thy heavy riches but a journey,
And Death unloads thee.

(9)   Friend hast thou none;
For thine own bowels which do call thee sire,
The mere effusion of thy proper loins,
Do curse the gout, serpigo, and the rheum,
For ending thee no sooner.

(10)   Thou hast nor youth nor age,
But, as it were, an after-dinner's sleep,
Dreaming on both; for all thy blessed youth
Becomes as aged, and doth beg the alms
Of palsied eld; and when thou art old and rich,
Thou hast neither heat, affection, limb, nor beauty,
To make thy riches pleasant. What's yet in this
That bears the name of life?

(11)   Yet in this life
Lie hid moe thousand deaths; yet death we fear,
That makes these odds all even.

And Claudio's reply to these arguments is equivalent to the conclusion of a formal piece of disputation:

> I humbly thank you.
> To seek to live, I find I seek to die;
> And seeking death find life. Let it come on.
> (MEASURE FOR MEASURE, III, i, 5–43)

Of course, it is possible to follow the Duke's reasoning without knowing how to analyse the lines in accordance with renaissance formal logic: but without analysing the speech, at least in such a way as to note what the Duke is doing, what his case is, and how he seeks to enforce it, we cannot hope to speak it properly. Nor can we hope to become identified with the Duke unless we follow his reasoning and try to prove his point as the proof has been unfolded in his mind. Some such analysis can help with that most awkward of speeches for the modern actor, the reply of the Archbishop of Canterbury to Henry V on the subject of Salic Law. The Archbishop's objective is to convince Henry that the law is in fact no bar to his claim to the French throne, and every word he speaks expresses a certainty that what he says is right. After the assertion that no possible bar can be brought forward but the Salic Law, he goes on to declare, and to prove, that it does not apply to France for two reasons. The first of these is that the 'Salique land' is not France, but the region of Germany known as Meissen; and even this region was not possessed by the French until 421 years after the death of the King to whom the Law was 'idly' ascribed. The second reason why the Law obviously cannot apply to France lies in the fact that the French Kings of the past

> all appear
> To hold in right and title of the female;
> So do the kings of France unto this day.

The conclusion to be drawn from all this is that the French

52

are using the Salic Law hypocritically but ineffectively as a weapon against Henry. (*Henry V*, I, ii, 32–95.) It is possible that the Archbishop does not really believe in his own case, but simulates belief in it to embroil the King in the French adventure. But even so the actor playing the part still has to understand how the argument is built up; he must still be able to run from one point to another, to turn back to emphasize one more heavily, as if the ideas were coming to expression in his own mind.

There is no need to know the names of the different stages in an argument in order to distinguish the relation of each to the others, and to notice how the thought and emotion progress from stage to stage. But the actor should be able to understand how the author has arranged the progression of ideas in the orderly manner which makes them most effective. To trace this structure is only the first step, of course; but it is by first following closely the way in which the meaning is expressed and arranged in successive stages of development that we can come to think, feel and want as the character does successively. Later the actor will utilize his first bare analysis to give a richer and deeper impersonation. Shakespeare has embodied the thoughts and emotions of his imagined character in an artificial structure, which nevertheless expresses feelings which are truthful and natural. The easiest way to act them truthfully and naturally is to make the poet's artificial structure the foundation of the performance. Indeed, it is already the foundation of the character's thoughts and desires as Shakespeare has imagined them. For instance, Cymbeline's justification of himself, passionate and full of feeling as it is, is none the less logical and orderly in its construction; first comes the triple assertion:

> Mine eyes
> Were not in fault, for she was beautiful;
> Mine ears, that heard her flattery; nor my heart,
> That thought her like her seeming.

He can now come to the next stage of his argument:

>   It had been vicious
> To have mistrusted her:

And it is possible for him to proceed from this point to the admission which he is prepared to make, and which is in itself an excuse:

>   yet, O my daughter!
> That was folly in me thou mayst say,
> And prove it in thy feeling.

> (CYMBELINE, V, v, 62–68)

In every case, whether it is of small units or large, of figures of words or whole speeches, the importance of structural analysis lies in the fact that it leads us into an understanding of the character without diminishing the power of the poetry. Indeed, it allows us to apprehend all the more easily as an imaginary human being, who seems to be really alive, the character which has been poetically created by the author.

The emphasis of this chapter has been so great on a process of intellectualization as possibly to suggest that this is regarded as of greatest importance in preparing and in acting a role. Perhaps by calling attention to an aspect of Shakespeare which gets too little attention, the impression has been given quite unintentionally that intellectual analysis is regarded as of greater importance than creative imagining, than the feeling of sincere emotion and the striving after an objective. But this impression should be resisted. Intellectual analysis has its place at some stage of preparation; but at what stage and to what extent the analysis is required varies with every individual. And there are actors who never need to make a conscious analysis of sense and structure, because they have already developed independently a subconscious awareness of the relation between words, sense and their own intonations.

Three

SPEAKING THE SCORE

THE PROBLEM OF SPEAKING Shakespeare's score is two-fold; on the one hand the actor has to give his audience an experience of the lines as poetry, and on the other he must sound natural, like a real human being putting his thoughts and feelings, his intentions and desires, into the words; these must come from the actor's mouth as if they had just arisen to express his thoughts and feelings, his intentions and desires, in his mind.

The poetry of Shakespeare which the actor has to make his audience experience can itself be regarded broadly as a combination of two elements; first there is the sense of the lines fused with the implications arising from it in its context; and second there is the melody which derives from the structure of the line or lines as an organization of articulate sound by which the sense and its implications are expressed.

A line spoken by Lady Macbeth serves admirably to illustrate this working definition of what we call 'the poetry':

That which hath made them drunk hath made me
    bold.

                               (II, ii, 1)

Here the sense is simple and is expressed precisely; it can be paraphrased, and, taken out of its context, will continue to say that something which has made them drunk has made me bold. But in its context in the play the line's full meaning is much more than its sense; the meaning involves implications, among which is the character's emotion. 'Them' refers to the grooms and 'me' to the speaker, Lady Macbeth. They have been tricked, and she has tricked them; they are the losers, she is the victor; she feels them to be contemptible and negligible, she feels herself to be splendid and very much to be reckoned with. She is elated by the fact that the drink has prevented them from behaving in accordance with their nature, their manhood, if it were allowed to function properly; it can no longer keep harm from the unguarded Duncan. The elation is intensified by the other side of the picture; the drink has prevented her, a woman, from behaving in accordance with her nature if it were functioning properly; no longer can womanly softness prevent her from bringing harm to the King. Indeed, at this moment she feels capable of the murder herself. These implications arise from the context, for earlier Lady Macbeth has asked to be unsexed so that she may have the relentless, remorseless hardness of a man; and later she will declare that if Duncan had not resembled her father as he slept, she would have killed him herself. It is valid to presume, therefore, that as she speaks this particular line she is exulting in her new feeling of being utterly capable of killing the King if need be. And what gives the utmost exhilaration to her triumph, what is most exquisitely delightful for her to contemplate in the situation, is the fact that in each case the good work has been done by the same thing, the drink; it has made the grooms other than men; it has made her other than woman. The success of her plan depends upon these changes taking place simultaneously; they have, and she anticipates her triumph with her elation. There is no intention here of suggesting that this is a difficult line needing intricate explication if its obscurities are to be clear to everybody. In fact, of course, the line is clear; and to many readers what has been said about it up to this point may be so obvious as not to need saying at all. The point of analysing this line, however, is not to explicate it, but, because it is not obscure, to make use of it as an illustration of what ought to be said about the needs which must be answered in speaking it. Simply because this line presents no intellectual and emotional difficulties it serves well as an illustration of each of the processes involved in speaking Shakespeare successfully.

To speak her line so that the audience experiences its poetry, then, the actress has not only to speak the sense but to convey these complex implications; and it may well be asked how much of this task she can be expected to accomplish in fact. Thanks both to the nature of acting as an art, and to the way in which Shakespeare has written in the renaissance tradition which we have examined, it is possible for an actor or actress to speak his sense and think and feel its implications; and then most, if not all, of the meaning can be conveyed.

The task is made easier by the fact that the poet has expressed what is a complex meaning by means of precise arrangements of sense. However imprecise and complex the implications may be, the sense itself, the explicit part of the meaning, is precise and simple. If we examine the verbal patterning in which the sense is expressed we see three important relationships:

That which *hath made* (1) *them* (2) *drunk* (3) *hath made* (1) *me* (2) *bold* (3).

The figures into which the sense has been organized and which must be 'made manifest' are as follows: the ploche, 'hath made'—'hath made', the antithesis, 'them'—'me', and the balancing (almost an antithesis), 'drunk'—'bold'.

When it comes to speaking this line the emphasis must be distributed in such a way that the relationship in which these words have been organized as sense is transmitted to the listener in a pattern of sound. To let the listener hear these individual patterns as they are interwoven in the text does not, however, make any demands which the human voice is incapable of satisfying: the speaker can succeed if she does not rely solely upon stress—that is, percussion—but if she combines with it changes both of pitch and length. As a result her voice will go up and down in pitch, and its tones will be longer or shorter as the sense requires. The words 'stress' and 'emphasis' are often used synonymously; in the sense in which it is used here, however, stress is restricted to percussion, the difference between a stressed and an unstressed syllable; but emphasis is the use of the voice to express sense whether by stress, by change of pitch or by change of length. Stress is merely one of the three kinds of emphasis.

Every actress is free to choose for herself the actual changes of voice by means of which her emphasis will make manifest the sense pattern of the line, 'That which hath made them drunk hath made me bold'. The metrical pattern demands a stress (percussion) upon 'That', 'made', 'drunk', 'made', 'bold'; but each individual is at liberty to find her own way of emphasizing 'them' and 'me'. Whatever inflexions she may employ, however, their effect must be both to isolate the words and show them in their relationship to one another in a unit whose connexion with the rest of the line is also apparent. One possible way, but by no means the only way, of emphasizing these words to obtain this result is to give 'them' a high note which will be answered by a lower note for 'me'. Similarly the relation between 'drunk' and 'bold' can be shown by the use of a low note for the first and of a higher note for the second of these two words. 'Hath made'—'hath made' presents no difficulty inasmuch as clear enunciation automatically creates the pattern of the same sounds in repetition for the listening ear.

This is only one of the possible ways of emphasizing the words in the line to convey its sense. Every actress of the part will find her own way of making the sense 'manifest'; her actual inflexions will be those which are right for her voice and her personality when speaking this sense; but the sense itself will be the same, whatever the inflexion employed to emphasize it.

Of course, in acting this line or any other, no actress or actor will try to reproduce any pattern of sound or of sense as such. Identified with the character, the performer concentrates on wanting to express what that character wants. What the actress of Lady Macbeth will do with her voice will be the result of her wanting to say what Lady Macbeth has been imagined by Shakespeare as wanting to say. Nevertheless, the actress's ability to say this as it ought to be said, as it has been expressed in this particular line of verse, will depend very much upon technical preparation at some stage of her study.

It is the technical preparation with which we are concerned here. A preparatory analysis of the line shows the relationships between the various words, and leads to a consideration of what is technically involved in speaking them. After the details of emphasis have been worked out they can become forgotten by the unconscious mind at that stage of preparation in which technique becomes second nature. In acting the role the actress will never aim at reproducing figures or structural patterns, nor does she need to be aware of them consciously as such. If she thinks of sound linked to sound and word linked to word she must fail. But because she thought consciously of such points at some stage of preparation she will now be able to concern herself solely with what ought always to be her sole concern in acting, the speaking in the person of the character what that character wants to say.

That part of the meaning of 'That which hath made them drunk hath made me bold' which has been expressed explicitly and precisely as sense can be conveyed by emphasis which consists of stresses, changes of pitch and changes of

length. But there is still the task of transmitting the imprecise and complex implications, each of which may be precisely and separately formulated explicitly as we ponder
over the line, but which lose their precision as we relate
them to the sense and are aware of them, more or less simultaneously, as meaning. It is here that the art of acting
triumphs. The actress, while speaking with an emphasis
which embodies the explicit sense in a pattern of intonations, thinks and feels what it implies. She has pondered the
complexities of the meaning when preparing her performance; then she was able to do what the reader does, but
what cannot be done in actual performance; she could stop
and think, look back and forward in the play until each line
was seen and understood, not merely as sense, but as meaning in its context. So that when she actually performs the
role, the implications have been related clearly to the units
of words which convey the sense. Now she uses her imagination; what those of us who do not force our souls to our own
conceit are aware of as an intellectual knowledge of what
the character wants is experienced imaginatively by the
actress as if she were the character. Thinking, feeling and
wanting as if she were Lady Macbeth, she will transmit the
meaning in her voice. The structural relationships will be
apparent, the figures will be 'made manifest', but not because she consciously thinks of structural relationships of
sound and sense as something to be reproduced in her performance. She will have considered them at some stage of
preparation, with the result that now her whole endeavour
will be to express all that Lady Macbeth wants by means of
this line.

To some extent the audience will be given an explicit
statement; but that part of the meaning which is not explicit to the reader will be implied in her manner and her
tones, for all that it is complex. Her appearance, her face and
movements will have a part to play; but this aspect of her
art will be considered in a later chapter; here we are con

cerned with what can be accomplished by speaking alone. From the voice the audience can be enabled to experience as poetry the bare sense fused to her feeling of triumph, her contempt for the grooms, her satisfaction with herself, her delight in the neat way in which the one drink is serving two complementary purposes. Of course she will not say explicitly that 'them' refers to persons negligible as men, nor that she herself has been endowed with strength to do things beyond the nature of women. But when she speaks 'them' and 'me' thinking of drunkenness and of her own boldness respectively, feeling contemptuous and superior, her audience will share her implications as they receive her explicit sense. So long as the actress feels herself endowed with a courage and hardness unnatural to a woman, she will sound like one with these qualities to her audience; there will be an electricity and tension in her speaking that will stir her listeners with a full understanding of what the poet has put into his line even if they cannot explicitly say what that is.

It is when the actress speaks the full meaning of the line that her voice takes on its full melody, the second element in what an audience experiences as 'poetry'. Basically the music comes from clear and correct enunciation of vowels and consonants as such, irrespective of their contribution to sense, occurring in a particular order. Emerging from this order, and created by it, are heard such repetitive patterns of sound as alliteration, assonance, rhyme, ploche and anaphora, which exist as figures solely in virtue of their sound. They can carry sense, of course, but they are what they are solely as patterns of sound.

Clear enunciation of Lady Macbeth's line, 'That which hath made them drunk hath made me bold', is enough to transmit the alliteration of *th*, *m* and *d*; the listener will hear the assonance of the sound of *a* in 'made'—'made', and of its sound in 'that'—'hath'—'hath'. The figure of ploche emerges from these details in the repetitions 'hath made'—'hath made'. Enunciation can also let the listener respond to the reversal of *tha* in 'that' into *ath* in 'that'.

This music combines with that demanded of inflexion by the sense pattern with its changes of pitch and length as well as stress. The relationship of words to one another as sense thus creates a pattern of intonation which counterpoints against the metrical pattern of stressed and unstressed syllables. In Lady Macbeth's line we have seen already that the following syllables are stressed: That, made, drunk, made, bold. But the sense pattern demands that in addition to the stress placed on 'drunk' and 'bold', they shall be linked to one another by emphasis of another kind, such as a lower pitch for 'drunk' and a higher for 'bold'. And sense again demands that 'them' and 'me', neither of which bears a stress, shall be distinguished in emphasis; in this case a higher pitch for 'them' was suggested as one satisfactory way, linked to a lower pitch for 'me'. This counterpointing of sense pattern against metrical pattern produces the rhythm of the line to some extent. Its full rhythm, however, like the rest of the melody, depends upon what happens to the voice when the imagination of the actress is involved in expressing the implications.

What occurs with this line of Lady Macbeth's is true of Shakespeare's verse as a whole; to scan him we take notice only of stress; but when we think his lines or speak them as sense, we blend the metrical pattern of stressed and unstressed syllables with the patterns of intonation created by the verbal structure. It is true also that prose involves the blending of intonation patterns with a series of stressed and unstressed syllables; but there is no recurring metrical pattern as in verse. If we consider Rosalind's lines of prose, for instance, we see that the sense expressed in the italicized words produces a pattern of inflexion:

no sooner *look'd* but they *lov'd*; no sooner *lov'd* but they *sigh'd*; no sooner *sigh'd* but they ask'd one another *the reason*; no sooner knew *the reason* but they sought *the remedy*.

Here the climax can be heard when spoken and expresses a relationship of sense in sound; but the pattern of intonation thus produced counterpoints against an irregular succession of stressed and unstressed syllables. In the climax spoken by Claudius, however, printed here as if it were prose, we have a regular succession of stressed and unstressed syllables blending with the intonations produced by the sense in this arrangement of words.

And let *the kettle* to *the trumpet* sound, *the trumpet* to *the cannoneer* without, *the cannons* to *the heavens, the heavens* to *the earth*.

The lines quoted from Rosalind contain other figurative patterns in addition to that of climax. There are the various repetitions of 'no sooner', 'they' and 'but', and the balancing of 'asked'—'knew'—'sought'. But the intonation which makes the sense in these figures 'manifest' still does not have the rhythmic quality which is acquired when there is counterpointing with a metrical pattern. This rhythmic difference is apparent if we compare the antithetical pattern of the prose of the Doctor in *Macbeth* with that of the verse of Gratiano's lines in *The Merchant of Venice*.

A great perturbation in nature, *to receive* (1) at once *the benefit* (2) *of sleep*, (3) and *do* (1) *the effects* (2) *of watching!* (3) (v, i, 9–10.)

And let *my liver* (1) rather *heat* (2) *with wine* (3) Than *my heart* (1) *cool* (2) *with mortifying groans*. (3)

(I, i, 81–82)

These two extracts have similar patterns of intonation arising from the word arrangement which conveys the sense: in each case there are three units of linked equivalents: 'to receive'—'to do'; 'my liver'—'my heart': 'the benefit'—

63

'the effects'; 'heat'—'cool': 'of sleep'—'of watching'; 'with wine'—'with mortifying groans'. But the essential differ- ence of rhythm springs from the fact that Gratiano's lines have a metrical pattern of stressed and unstressed syllables, whereas the stresses in the Doctor's do not recur regularly. In these lines, whether they are verse or prose, full melody is produced only when the imagination of the speaker is involved in expressing the implications as well as the sense.

Emotion obviously plays a great part in producing the music of the line, giving colour and life to the tones re- quired by sense. Just as the sense must be understood precisely, however imprecise its implications as a whole, so the emotion must be felt precisely. The actor or actress must know and feel exactly what emotion derives from a particu- lar word or combination of words. Then, in the speaking of the lines, emotion may well change as precisely as the sense. In Lady Macbeth's line, for instance, 'That which hath made them drunk hath made me bold,' while the implica- tions of 'them' are not confined to contempt, this is the dominant emotion which will colour the actress's tone; and triumph will be expressed in 'me'. Similarly, while con- tempt, again, is attached to 'drunk', relentless courage is expressed by 'bold'. The precision of the sense and the emotion plays its part in producing the melody of the line again in the repetition of 'hath made': the second time she speaks these words the actress feels Lady Macbeth's enjoy- ment of the fact that the same drink has had two such opposing effects, with the result that the timbre and inten- sity of the second 'hath made' will be quite different from those of the first. Indeed, from emotion and the other implications of the sense of a line are derived those varia- tions of pace, pausing, volume, timbre, intensity, and tone which develop the full melody out of the foundation pro- vided by enunciation and emphasis. When the performer enunciates clearly and accurately, embodies sense in emphasis and thinks and feels the implications of the sense to give the full meaning, then the melody derives from the actual verbal structure. But this can be done only when the precise sense is understood and 'made manifest', when the emotion or emotions are felt precisely as well as strongly, and when the performer thinks and feels the implications of the sense powerfully.

An actress can give a poetry to Lady Macbeth's line if she is vaguely but powerfully affected by it herself. She may not perceive the precise interrelationship of words in a sense pattern which guides the reader and speaker towards an appreciation of the exact contrast between the grooms and the potential murderess who triumphs in their discomfiture; she may, however, feel very powerfully the character's elation in her newly acquired courage, and express this elation and courage so powerfully as to delight her audience with an experience of poetry, which will include the music of her voice. Nevertheless the poetry will be vague, if powerful, and the music will not be as varied as it is when it derives from the line structure. Her rhythm will not be the result of the blending of the metrical pattern with that pattern of intonation which makes the precise sense manifest. The music which Shakespeare's line ought to draw from any and every actress can only be produced when her inflexions are those which the precise and whole sense demands from her voice and personality, and when her pace, tones, intensity and timbre come from the implications of that sense. For the aim is to allow the melody to come from the meaning, a meaning in which the sense is always explicitly to be heard.

When this is done, not only will the actress have accomplished the first part of her task, which is to convey Shakespeare's poetry, but she will have triumphed in the second as well: she will sound natural. For the sense pattern and the emotions are expressed only, and yet adequately, by the normal tones of her speaking voice; they may have greater resonance and intensity than in her colloquial speaking, yet they will be exactly the tones which she will use colloquially to express the same sense and emotion. The actress or actor never needs to use any of the frequencies which do not occur in speaking, none of those which are produced by the human voice, for instance, in *recitativo secco*, *recitativo stromento*, or singing. There is no need for any sort of 'poetic' or 'incantatory' voice; the normal speaking voice, correctly produced and controlled, will always sound natural provided it is inflected to express the precise sense, and provided the performer feels the emotion precisely. Its music will not suffer from the fact that only the tones of the normal speaking voice are used; for verse is distinguished from colloquial prose not only by metre, but by that structural organization of words whose sense produces a more musical succession of changes of pitch and length. In this latter respect Shakespeare's prose, where it is patterned, agrees with verse in differing from colloquial speech; colloquial prose is not organized in a way which results in an emphasis of its sense producing such a variety of natural inflexions in a given number of words.

Indeed, the sense often demands so many changes of inflexion as to prompt the question whether too much is being asked of the actor's voice. In practice, however, I have found that a performer whose voice is competently produced can 'make manifest' Shakespeare's most complicated patterns of sense. While I would not wish to be dogmatic on this point, I would observe that in my experience Shakespeare is best and most easily spoken with what is called a sustained tone, depending on diaphragm support; when combined with clear and accurate enunciation, the sustained tone allows the actor to change pitch and length swiftly as well as precisely. It is important that he should be able to do this without losing pace; for while he does not always have to speak swiftly, there are times when he must. Pace ought to be varied according to the needs of his lines rather than in accordance with his mastery or lack of mastery of the technique underlying his art.

The point cannot be made too often, that the way for an actor both to sound natural and to give his audience an experience of the poetry of Shakespeare is to be found in conveying the explicit sense precisely in an emphasis whose inflexions make 'manifest' the arrangements of words, while at the same time he thinks and feels the implications. Moreover, among the implications is the emotions which must be felt as precisely as the sense is thought. One great difficulty for the actor lies in the fact that he can be affected powerfully by lines whose sense is not precisely explicit to him. When this happens he will often give a stirring and powerful performance, but it will not be the same as when he bases his acting on a clear understanding of Shakespeare's sense expressed in precise patternings of words. In changing or missing the sense the actor can easily miss some of Shakespeare's implications, and even miss some of the strengths or subtleties of characterization. Let us consider as an example of this difficulty the retort of Richard III at the beginning of the play when the gentleman tells him to stand back and let the bier pass:

> Advance thy halberd higher than my breast,
> Or, by Saint Paul, I'll strike thee to my foot.
>
> (I, ii, 40–41)

I have heard in practice an actor speak this line as if instead of 'Or', Richard had said 'And'. The result was to speak exactly the opposite sense to that which the line expresses. Richard was made to tell the man not to advance his halberd, where in fact he says to advance it. The lines were acted vigorously and Richard's pride and egoism were admirably embodied. Nevertheless, musical and vigorous as it was, the speaking missed both Shakespeare's music and his subtlety of characterization. If we analyse the lines we find four sets of equivalents: 'Advance'—'I'll strike'; 'thy halberd'—'thee'; 'higher than'—'to'; 'my breast'—'my foot'. It is also possible to argue that it would be more correct to separate 'I' from ''ll strike' and balance it against an understood 'you'. An actor who is aware of the precise sense of the words he is speaking here gives both a richer music and a richer meaning. Instead of saying virtually, 'Put that up and I'll knock you down,' he says, 'If you (1) don't (2) put that (3) up, I (1) am going to knock (2) you (3) down.' And in the contrast between the equivalents in the actual wording of the threat as Shakespeare gives it is a sardonic implication. Richard is enjoying a cat-and-mouse game; he delights in the thought, 'If that doesn't go up, you're going to go down.' And in this delight and the way in which he expresses it is revealed an important trait in his character.

Acting being the art which it is, an actor can easily move us with a sense and implications which do not really belong to the words which he is speaking. The better he is the more easily can he overwhelm us, for instance, merely by counting from one to ten. Then, whether he conveys the actual sense of the numbers or not, he can think and feel implications which arise from a context which he has imagined, perhaps from a sense which he has imagined as well. What he conveys to us will be his thinking and feeling of the implications which he has created for himself, and which he experiences powerfully. If an actor lacked this ability to experience and transmit his experience to others he would be useless in his art. But for all that, he has still to be careful not to imagine a line of precisely explicit sense with implications belonging to another sense. It is always within his power to do so, and his audience may well be delighted with the result. But both he and they will be happier when his sense is that of the line, and when his implications arise from it and do not conflict with the line's structure. For, by ignoring or conflicting with the structure of a line of precisely explicit sense, the actor is apt to distort its music. Again it is as if he were counting from one to ten and producing the most entrancing, stirring or heart-rending melody, simply by thinking his own sense, and by thinking and feeling his own implications. When he does this with Shakespeare, however, he does not give us a music which derives from the line, which can be related back to it, which we can experience as the line's poetry made actual in sound; instead, quite unintentionally and in all good faith, he gives us the melody arising from meaning which he has infused into the words which he is speaking, but which does not really relate to their explicit sense in its structure of words, and which is not really evoked by that sense in its context. Yet the art of speaking Shakespeare's score depends very much on the actor's ability to convey implications and sense as melody, on his ability to speak a line with the meaning which he has in his mind. This ability lies at the core of his art, and when applied to what Shakespeare has actually organized in a precise arrangement of words, it produces the most triumphant results. The melody of the actor's voice is a part of the full meaning which he expresses; it is a kind of musical thinking which is fused to that part of the meaning which is verbal thinking. And that provides another reason for producing from the line that music which its structure, its sense and implications ought to evoke from the voice and personality of the actor.

An actress can succeed in portraying the lifelike character and the poetry when speaking Lady Macbeth's line; and an actor can succeed equally well with a line such as Macbeth's:

> Whiles I threat, he lives.
> (II, ii, 60)

Here once more there is a simple and taut arrangement of sense in the units, 'I'—'he', 'threat'—'lives'. And in each of these passages, while the implications are complex compared with the sense from which they arise, they are simple when we compare them with those of many passages in Shakespeare on which commentators and critics have lavished interpretative ingenuity. Success in the simple examples does not necessarily mean equal success where the task is much more difficult.

But before we decide that Shakespeare has written much verse and prose whose poetry cannot be conveyed in the theatre, and which is accessible only when we have his text in front of us to read and think over, we need to consider why, in fact, he so often strikes us today as complex or obscure, and whether he really is simpler than he seems. Shakespeare's meaning is obscure not only when the sense has been lost beyond recall for all readers, but when it has changed. Sometimes when the sense has not changed it has different implications today; and obviously when the sense of a passage itself has changed since Shakespeare wrote it, it can now give rise to implications too complex to be conveyed by an actor in the theatre.

Where the sense of a word or passage has been lost and experts disagree among themselves as to the probabilities of differing conjectures, then the actor must imagine both sense and implications for himself. A good example of this difficulty is provided by Hamlet's

> The dram of eale
> Doth all the noble substance of a doubt
> To his own scandal.

> (I, iv, 36–38)

Here the actor may be guided by one or other of the conjectural paraphrases of the sense; he may decide to read 'the dram of eale' as a sarcastic reference to Danish drunkenness ('the dram of ale') with a play on 'eale' in the sense 'evil'. He may substitute 'offer' for 'of a', yet the line will not take on that precise clarity of sense which we are usually justified in expecting. There is no alternative here to a powerful rendering of what it seems vaguely to be saying, that one fault in an otherwise perfect record can lead to the shaming of what would otherwise be regarded by men as

70

admirable. If the actor speaks this sense he will have implications which do not conflict with the rest of the speech, but
which round it off.

In cases such as this the rest of the speech can often be
taken as a guide to what must serve as a second-best substitute for the meaning which is now lost to us. When the
actor cannot find the sense of one or two words he will often
receive help from the rest of the rhythmic pattern to which
they belong. For instance, an actress who does not know the
exact sense of 'the receipt of reason' and 'a limbec' can still
give a creditable rendering of Lady Macbeth's

> That memory, the warder of the brain,
> Shall be a fume, and the receipt of reason
> A limbec only
>
> (I, vii, 65–67)

Knowing vaguely that a limbec is a utensil for alchemic
experiments and assuming, still vaguely, that the 'receipt
of reason' has some connexion with the brain receiving
reason, she can rely on the structure of the lines to guide
her. The pattern of the first statement is repeated in the
second. 'That memory shall be a fume' is a statement 'that
this shall be that', and requires an inflexion which makes
that sense clear. Similarly, even if we do not know the precise sense of the second statement, it still has the shape of
'and this (the receipt of reason) shall be that (a limbec only)'.
Something can then be made of the passage by assuming
that the second statement is an intensification of the first.

In actual fact the second statement is an intensifying of
the first. It ceases to be obscure, moreover, when we know
that 'the receipt of reason' is 'the receptacle of reason',
literally the cranium; and that a limbec is not merely an
alchemical retort of vague use, but one which was actually
used to reduce solids to vapours. We now see that Lady
Macbeth is exulting in the thought that the drink which

71

she will give to the grooms will not merely make them forget their duty, turning memory into a vapour, but the very
cranium itself will be converted into a piece of apparatus
whose purpose is to reduce solids to vapours.

But what is the good of our actress knowing this if her
audience does not? She cannot provide them with a glossary
to make certain that they will know the sense of her words,
it is true; yet if she knows the sense, her speaking of the
implications will be much more convincing and rich in
poetry; and her audience will be so affected by the implications as not to notice their ignorance of the sense. They will
be stirred by something whose sense is obscure but whose
meaning is powerfully accessible to them. Something of the
same sort happens with a word whose sense has changed,
such as 'presently'. Our actor who knows that Hamlet is
saying 'immediately' cannot stop and tell his audience not
to think that the sense is 'in a little while' or 'not immediately'. But he can speak and act 'presently' in its sense of
'immediately' so that all his audience know that he expects
Claudius to betray himself there and then while watching
the Mouse-trap:

> guilty creatures, sitting at a play,
> Have by the very cunning of the scene
> Been struck so to the soul that presently
> They have proclaim'd their malefactions.

(II, ii, 585–8)

In the cases which we have considered so far, changes of
sense have not led to complexities of implication which
throw too great a burden on the actor. But the lines spoken
by Polixenes to Hermione at the beginning of *The Winter's
Tale* seem very obscure and complicated if we do not read
'blood' and 'spirit' in their precise Jacobean sense.

> We were as twinn'd lambs that did frisk i' th' sun
> And bleat the one at th' other. What we chang'd

Was innocence for innocence; we knew not
The doctrine of ill-doing, nor dream'd
That any did. Had we pursu'd that life,
And our weak spirits ne'er been higher rear'd
With stronger blood, we should have answer'd heaven
Boldly 'Not guilty', the imposition clear'd
Hereditary ours.

(I, ii, 67–75)

Here 'spirits' is used in the sense in which we find it in renaissance physiology to denote the substance which was believed to be both body and soul and which permeated the body penetrating every part of it with the blood. The theory postulated three different spirits, the natural, the vital and the animal; as substance which was both body and soul each of the spirits had a part to play as the link between the body and the soul. The soul itself was regarded as threefold, or as having three aspects. Of these, the Vegetable Soul, present also in plants, irrational creatures, animals, birds, fish, reptiles and insects, was served by the natural spirits, which were concocted out of the blood in the liver, and thence carried round the body to the organs of reproduction, growth and nourishment. Animals, reptiles, insects, birds and men also shared the second aspect of the human soul which was called the Sensible Soul; the link between this and the sense organs was provided by the vital spirits refined out of the natural spirits when they had mounted with the blood to the heart. But man alone of life created on the earth being the possessor of a Rational Soul, he alone possessed the third kind of spirits, the animal spirits which served as the link between the rational soul and the body. These spirits were refined out of the vital spirits in the brain to which these latter had mounted together with the blood. 'Spirits' and 'blood' are used by Polixenes in their literal senses of physiological spirits and blood respectively. His meaning involves the conceit that if they had stayed lambs they would not have had rational souls; then their blood would not have mounted higher from the heart to the brain to refine animal spirits to connect the body with the rational soul. As lambs rather than human beings they would not have shared in Original Guilt inherited from Adam by all his descendants. But as in fact these two boys grew up and their spirits were 'higher rear'd' with their 'stronger blood' as it ascended from heart to brain, they lost their innocence and could no longer give heaven the same bold answer.

For the actor with this knowledge of the basic sense the passage becomes simple. But unless his audience has been instructed in the Jacobean sense or is provided with a glossary to consult, it is doubtful if he will be able to convey it to them. Nevertheless, as the sense and its implications are no longer obscure to the actor he can transmit the implications, if not the precise sense, much more clearly and powerfully, and this is true of the emotion in particular. He is a man able to recall the innocent friendship of childhood, and childhood itself, as possessing a quality which has now gone. There is a wistfulness but not a bitterness in his admission with its witty recognition of what he sees as reality. He has not yet learned how much deeper and more violent the change has been than he supposes at this moment. And at this point we see that when discussing the implications of the sense in different passages of Shakespeare we have to distinguish between those which exist for the character and those existing for his creator and audience. For Polixenes, the implications are that in the nature of things he and Leontes could not play so carelessly and innocently once they grew up. But for the audience there is an introduction to one of the themes of the play, that sin and error are inescapable in human life, but that, thanks to a benevolent Providence, repentance can avoid their worst consequences and lead to a state of reconciliation in which the lost harmonies of youth with its freshness can rejuvenate what has been stained and faded with age and sin. The actor makes

us aware of the introduction of this theme, not by trying to
include it in his meaning, but by giving us simply the meaning which there is for Polixenes. This meaning in its context
makes us aware of the developing of the theme.

To know the precise sense again is to dissipate the obscurity and with it a complexity of implication which defies the
actor in the theatre in the case of Macbeth's lines:

> My thought, whose murder yet is but phantastical,
> Shakes so my single state of man
> That function is smother'd in surmise,
> And nothing is but what is not.

(I, iii, 138–41)

Macbeth is saying that although his thought harbours a
murder as yet only imaginary (phantastical), it so shatters
the unified state of being a man that his ability to move, to
make use of the organs dependent upon the sensible soul,
has been nullified by imagining (surmise), with the result
that nothing exists for him but something which he realizes
is as yet no more than imaginary. 'My single state of man'
is an insistence upon the fact that in human beings physical
body and spiritual soul are not two separate entities tied
together, but one unified state of both body and soul inter-
penetrating one another. So violent is the effect of what he
imagines that this union has been nullified and his body is
left as if it had no soul to enable it to function; similarly
soul is left as if it had no body. Moreover in this ecstasy he
finds the real scene in which he stands there on the heath
with his companions less real to him than that of the murder
which he imagines as if it were actually before him,
although he knows it is only imaginary. Nothing exists for
him except something which he knows does not really exist.
It is important that we should see that Macbeth himself can
distinguish between the real and the imaginary, but that his
ability to do so makes no difference to the effect of the
imaginary upon his 'single state of man'. He is in the same

situation later when he hears the knocking on the door, and, although he knows exactly what it is, he is nevertheless affected by it as if it were a supernatural summons.

> Whence is that knocking?
> How is't with me, when every noise appals me?
>
> (II, ii, 57–58)

Again he can distinguish rationally between appearance and reality, but knowing the reality he is nevertheless overwhelmed by its effect on his imagination. This is only a noise of knocking, but it literally appals him; and although self-preservation should make him hurry off to wash, he stands there unable to move, 'lost so poorly' in his thoughts.

A different problem is presented to the actor by lines whose sense has not changed, but whose implications have, or whose implications are quite hidden today, although they were clear when the poet was writing. The sense of Macbeth's words is still the same as when the first actor of the part shuddered, 'As they had seen me with these hangman's hands.' But the implications have changed, inasmuch as the hangman no longer draws his victim's entrails and then quarters him. Nevertheless an actor who knows the implications, who thinks and feels them, will have no difficulty in conveying his shame at the ignoble butcher's work he has just executed, especially if he lets his audience see his hands smeared with blood.

Lear's words about Poor Tom give us an example of sense whose implications are completely hidden until we have been provided with what was not uncommon knowledge in Shakespeare's day. The King refers to Tom as 'this philosopher', then as a 'learned Theban', actually addresses him as 'Noble philosopher', speaks of him again as 'my philosopher' and finally bids him, 'Come, good Athenian' (III, iv, 150–76). At first Tom is living proof for Lear that man's life is cheap as beast's. Bitterly disillusioned of his assumption that material splendour is the same as human dignity,

76

the King now sees the Bedlam as one of those ancient philosophers interpreted as denying that there is any essential difference between man and animal, and asserting that they are separated only by superficial trappings. But the reference to 'this same learned Theban' shows a change taking place in the old man's mind. For there was a 'learned Theban', one Epaminondas, who is mentioned in Humfrey Gifford's *Posy of Gillowflowers* (1580) as a man of noble birth, who like Socrates and others in the past, endured poverty with no trace of resentment. Epaminondas was learned; when the progress of his education had exhausted the resources of his native city, a teacher was found for him in Lysis of Tarentum. North's translation of Plutarch declares: 'his poverty was not dainty to him, because his parents were ever poor, and yet for all that he passed over it more easily by the study of philosophy.' Lear's mind flickers towards the realization that there is a philosophy which might prove a balm against his own afflictions, and Tom is to him one learned in both its theory and its practice. But the King goes yet farther with his address, 'good Athenian'. Now he has in his mind a recollection of the attitude and example of Socrates, who was reconciled not only to poverty, but to stripping himself of life itself, in the most perfect and unembittered resignation.

There is admittedly no possibility of the actor of Lear enabling his audience to share this information with him; but he can most powerfully convey to them the results of this succession of ideas in the King's mind. From the bitter insistence that man is no more in essence than a Bedlam, with the cry 'Off, off you lendings' as Lear identifies himself with a travesty of humanity, he has progressed to a more balanced acceptance and recognition of reality. The change shows itself in his manner; he is calmer, the violent satirical tone has gone, there is momentarily a real humility and most pathetic respect for Tom as one who has a true lesson to teach, who sets the finest of examples to be followed. The change develops with the progression from philosopher to learned Theban, to noble philosopher, to good Athenian, and shows the development of a spirit in Lear not so very far from that of his calm and joyous renunciation of the world in his 'Come, let's away to prison' at the end of the play. (V, iii, 8.) To portray this change is simple for an actor who himself knows the significance of the references to the philosophers; and in showing his audience the change, he will allow them to apprehend the implications of the incident itself in Shakespeare's vision of the play as a whole. Symbolically Lear is shown recognizing what humanity is in essence at last, and preparing to identify himself with it, instead of with its travesty. To identify the essential quality of man either with material wealth and splendour, or with the animal apparently left naked when the trappings are removed, is to travesty man in each case. But to communicate this to us symbolically the actor must act as if he really were Lear with his mind ranging for consolation over his memories of the philosophers of the past as he sees the pitiful wretch on the heath.

Earlier in this chapter passages have been discussed in which Shakespeare has expressed his sense in patternings of words easily spoken as patterns of sound. In each case the actor's task was shown to be simplified when he makes his recognition of this precise sense, superficial as it may be, the foundation of his performance. Even in passages not built up in figures of words, however, a recognition of the precise sense is essential for real success. Macbeth's vision of the cosmos outraged against him does not involve verbal patterning of the kind which he uses at the beginning of the speech, but an understanding of the precise sense is still the key to the most successful rendering. The powerful complexity of this vision is bound up with the images; but they, complex as they are, individually and as a whole, are revealed as a logical succession of ideas when their surface sense is mastered. Duncan has worn the powers of his office with such mildness, without arrogance, and has been so guiltless, despite the temptations and opportunities of such a position,

> that his virtues
> Will plead like angels, trumpet-tongu'd, against
> The deep damnation of his taking-off;
> And pity, like a naked new-born babe,
> Striding the blast, or heaven's cherubin hors'd
> Upon the sightless couriers of the air,
> Shall blow the horrid deed in every eye,
> That tears shall drown the wind.
>
> (I, vii, 18–25)

Macbeth has been considering his own judgement, 'here'. This will come before he is dead; he will not be allowed to put it off until Doomsday. And when it comes, his sins will speak against him, particularly those of killing a kinsman who is his king, and of killing a guest whose life he should fight to preserve. But their witness will be supported simultaneously by the plea made for Duncan by his own virtues. Duncan will also have his judgement before Doomsday; then his virtues will plead before the court against his being damned because he has been so treacherously killed in his sleep by one whom he trusted. What speaks for Duncan in these circumstances must necessarily add to the case against Macbeth. Anticipating Gabriel's trumpet, Duncan's virtues will arouse the world to horror and pity now. The trumpet-tongued pleading of the virtues (pleading in the sense of begging mercy as well as speaking to a brief in law) will bring pity like a naked new-born babe astride the blast, the stream of air coming from the virtues' pleading as from trumpets. The image of a naked new-born baby changes quite naturally into one of the cherubin,[1] for while these

---

[1] The form 'cherubin' used here is a normal singular, which may easily be mistaken for a plural owing to its similarity to the plural 'cherubim'—'cherubs'. Shakespeare uses 'heaven's cherubin' in an image of one, not of more than one, cherub riding on the invisible winds.

are sometimes shown in painting as babies' heads with wings but no body, they are also shown as winged chubby babies. In the transition from the image of pity to that of heaven's cherubin, Shakespeare has imagined Macbeth having a vision of something like what is painted in Romeo's lines:

> O, speak again, bright angel, for thou art
> As glorious to this night, being o'er my head,
> As is a winged messenger of heaven
> Unto the white-upturned wond'ring eyes
> Of mortals that fall back to gaze on him,
> When he bestrides the lazy-pacing clouds
> And sails upon the bosom of the air.
>
> (ROMEO AND JULIET, II, ii, 26–32)

A cherubin is also a bright angel, and as an angel of light is particularly terrible to Macbeth. But instead of bestriding lazy-pacing clouds, Macbeth's naked baby rushes swiftly and shatteringly on the trumpet's blast. Either pity looking like a cherub, or the actual cherubin of heaven, horsed, not on the blast from the pleading, but on the winds, the sightless couriers of the air, will blow an awareness of the horrid deed in every eye; and when this is done, with Macbeth exposed and with every eye shedding tears of pity for what it sees, the rain of tears drowns the wind. Quite logically the passage ends at the point where the virtues, which have set out to save Duncan by preventing his damnation, cease pleading, their end being achieved. With an end to their pleading, there is an end to the trumpet blast, tears have drowned the wind.

There is much more to the full meaning of this passage than has been suggested here, but an actor who understands the sense as here paraphrased with some of the implications, will have a simpler task, both in portraying Macbeth at this moment and in making his audience experience the poetry.

80

Verse speaking is a matter of expressing the sense and its implications and of producing melody. Both melody and meaning are inseparable from the structure of words in which they are both embodied. In the actual speaking, emphasis is varied in order to 'make manifest' the precise sense, while the imagining of the implications gives a greater depth and complexity, out of which the music of the line is produced as a matter of course.

Obviously, much can be done with the voice alone to give the audience an experience of poetry while sounding natural and while perfectly in character; but still more can be achieved by the full acting which includes movement, attitude, appearance and everything by means of which meaning can be expressed through the body. Ideally acting is a suiting of the action to the word; it is an imaging both in voice and body of all that is expressed in the word. This chapter has considered the use of the voice in speaking the score; in the next the Elizabethan attitude to the imaging of meaning in the body will be discussed, once again with a view to suggesting ways in which renaissance principles may be applied profitably today.

Four

ACTION AND THE WORD

THE PROBLEM OF SUITING the action to the word is no more than another aspect of that which faces the actor in speaking the score. Now he has not only to sound but to appear, to stand, move, behave as if he were the very person imagined by the dramatist, just as that person would be if he were to come to life. Nevertheless the words which Shakespeare has given his actor to speak would not be spoken by anybody in real life outside the theatre; and while they express truthfully the wishes and the character of the 'person of the drama', they remain the unrealistic lines written by the dramatist who has imagined that person. Real and truthful as the emotions are in themselves, and real and vital as the character himself is, this reality, truth and life have been imagined and created in terms of an unrealistic art. This means that the character and his emotions have to be played with truth and reality, yet with a truth and reality which do not clash with Shakespeare's medium of unrealistic words, whether these happen to be rhyme, blank verse or prose. Instead of clashing with the unrealistic medium, the truth and reality of the emotions and the characterization ought to develop from what has been expressed in it. As a result the actor must still present to us what seems to be a real human being with whom he has identified himself, and whose emotion must be, not merely seem, real and truthful; but he must also harmonize with the quality of his text, he must embody it, extending words with action, and never obscure their quality or depart from their spirit in his style of acting. But this is not to say that he is ever to give us anything which will ring untrue to the nature of the character which he is portraying, or anything which is in any way a falsification of the truth and reality of the emotions which Shakespeare has imagined.

It is not good enough to move back and fore between a realistic and an unrealistic style; there must be a homogeneous fusion of the realistic and the unrealistic which suits Shakespeare's expression of the real and true by means of an unrealistic medium. For Shakespeare cannot be acted satisfactorily by an actor who attends to no more than one of these elements at any one time. Shakespeare's actor must be identified, must present emotion and character truthfully and with reality, and yet he must always embody his lines, must always 'make manifest' their quality as literature which expresses emotion and character in specific situations. And we can learn from the Elizabethans here again much that will help us; what the renaissance rhetoricians have to tell us about the art of Alleyn, Burbage and their fellows can guide us when it comes to performing the lines which they acted so successfully in the age in which the plays were written.

When the modern actor is asked to take notice of accounts of 'rhetorical action' written by men such as John Bulwer and Abraham Fraunce, he may well hesitate and ask what can rhetoricians possibly have to tell us about the acting of stage-players in any age. After all, these writings are not specifically on stage-playing, but treat something which, however near allied to that art in some respects, strikes the modern mind as fundamentally unlike stage-playing as we know it, and as we suspect it to have been practised in Shakespeare's own theatre. 'Rhetorical delivery' suggests something too formal, something too stereotyped to allow of the deep and truthful characterization which Shakespeare demands. The rhetoricians' art strikes the modern who does not understand it as it existed in the renaissance as a matter of applying conventional gestures externally, whereas real acting is a matter of expressing what is felt from within. No two actors ought to be asked to express the same emotion in exactly the same way; and for this reason, the modern argument runs, an art which actually relies upon a conventional system of gestures to be applied always in the same way for the same emotion may obviously have been practised by orators, but could never have suited stage-players in Shakespeare's day, and certainly does not suit them now.

This argument would certainly be justified against turning to the rhetoricians for hints on how to act Shakespeare if in fact 'rhetorical delivery' had really been the conventional system of stereotyped gestures so forcefully denounced. But fortunately for us in our problem of fusing the realistic with the unrealistic, the art of the orator in the renaissance was anything but formal and stereotyped; on the contrary, it was a lively and truthful art designed to portray real emotion truthfully, and was based on a deep conviction that 'action' should spring always from real inner feeling, not from any conventional system of external clichés. Modern misapprehension of his enthusiasm often misrepresents John Bulwer as an advocate of formal and conventional gesture who believed that every speaker should express the same emotion in the same way. The best way of showing how far this is from what he really writes is to let him speak for himself. In the thirty-first of his 'Certain Cautionary Notions, extracted out of the ancient and modern rhetoricians', Bulwer insists:

In all action, nature bears the greatest sway: every man must consider his own nature and temperament. The reason is, because no man can put off his own, and put on another's nature. One action becomes one man, and another kind of behaviour, another. That which one does without art cannot wholly be delivered by art; for there is a kind of hidden and ineffable reason, which to know is the head of art. In some the civil virtues themselves [i.e. the details of the art of delivery] have no grace: in others, even the vices of rhetoric are comely and pleasing. Wherefore a rhetorician must know himself, yet not by common precepts; but he must take counsel of nature for the framing of the complexional and individual properties of his hand.[1]

'No man can put off his own, and put on another's nature' was an axiom never out of Bulwer's mind; and here in this passage he has given us one of the basic principles on which the art of the orator's action was established. Its other basic principles are no less reassuring to the modern anxious to understand not only what the art shared with stage-playing, but the way in which the Elizabethan player triumphed over the problem which confronts us, a problem which probably did not even exist for him as such at all. For although very little has come down to us about the actual art of the Elizabethan actor, we can turn with confidence for information on it to the comparatively copious accounts of rhetorical acting; for rhetorical delivery was derived largely from stage-playing. We are thus in a position to distinguish the basic principles of Elizabethan acting, to compare them with actual details of technique, and then to draw from them both guidance and inspiration in our own task today. For not only are the Elizabethan principles still valid, but Elizabethan practice offers examples which might well be adopted, and suggests to us what we might evolve to suit our own conditions when fusing the realistic and the unrealistic in a style fitted not only to Shakespeare's text, but to the actors and audiences of today.

[1]*Chironomia* (1644), p. 143.

85

The truth about rhetorical acting has been so often obscured or ignored that there is no harm in repeating yet again that the orators did not convert the art which they derived from stage-playing into a formal stereotyped code; their 'action' was not like the gesture of ballet or of Indian dancing; movement and gestures did not have arbitrary meanings, but expressed emotion in a way in which it was actually expressed outside the theatre; and they suited the style and the structure of the words which were spoken, once more in a way which was to be encountered as a matter of course in the real world of men. When it suited itself to the word, this action was precise, explicit and self-explanatory in the culture and society in which it flourished.

Bulwer and the other practitioners of rhetorical delivery subscribed wholeheartedly to the assertion of Thomas Wright that 'the fountain and origin of all external actions' must be 'the passion which is in our breast'.[1] Indeed, Bulwer was so enthusiastic about the hand and arms in 'action' because what they expressed so adequately came from 'the pathetical motions of the mind'. He declares that the movements of the hands 'show the mental springs from whence they naturally arise.'[2]

For Bulwer, gesture was not an external convention imposed from without; it was really nothing more or less than a satisfying of the need to express adequately something felt within. This is clear, for instance, in his handling of the gesture which he calls *Chirothripsia*, which is 'to press hard and wring another's hand'. To wring another's hand is to hold it between the palms, interlacing the fingers round it. 'This gesture,' says Bulwer, 'as it is a token of duty and reverential love, Coriolanus used towards his mother, Volumnia, when, overcome by her earnest persuasions to withdraw his army from Rome, he cried out, "Oh, Mother! What have you done to me?" ' As he speaks these words,

[1]T. Wright, *op. cit.*, p. 174.
[2]*Chirologia* (1644), p. 157; *Chiron.*, p. 16.

86

Coriolanus is described as 'holding her hard by the right hand'.[1] Bulwer gives Plutarch as his authority; and although this source does not actually say that Coriolanus wrung his mother's hand in this manner as a 'token of duty and reverential love', the incident is described almost exactly as Bulwer gives it to us.

> And with these words, herself, his wife and children, fell down upon their knees before him. Martius, seeing that, could refrain no longer, but went straight and lifted her up, crying out, 'Oh, Mother, what have you done to me?' And holding her hard by the right hand, 'Oh, Mother,' said he, 'You have won a happy victory for your country.'[2]

It has often been noticed that Shakespeare used North's Plutarch as a source for his treatment of this moment in the play, *Coriolanus*. As Volumnia falls silent, the First Folio has a stage direction, *Holds her by the hand silent*, before Coriolanus breaks out with the words, 'Mother, Oh Mother,' going on to confess that she has vanquished him. While Shakespeare's visualizing of this incident agrees with those of Bulwer and Plutarch, there is no certainty at all that the first actor of the role in the Shakespearian company did in fact hold his mother by the hand silently in the manner described as *Chirothripsia*. Yet it would have been possible for him to do so; he would have been able to express spontaneously in the movement the change of mind taking place even as he was deciding to avow his relationship to her and submit. In his mind he would have admitted to himself, and in his 'action' to the world, that he had been wrong to repudiate her and Rome.

A modern actor could express this complexity of inner feeling by the way in which he merely takes her hand in

[1]*Chirol.*, pp. 116; 118 f.
[2]Plutarch, *The Life of Caius Martius Coriolanus*, tr. North (1579), repr. W. J. Craig and R. H. Case, *The Tragedy of Coriolanus* (1922), p. lx.

one of his, and the same method was obviously open to an Elizabethan; yet this Elizabethan might really have wrung her hand in the manner described by Bulwer, simply because, in the tradition in which he lived and acted, to do so was as truthful a way of expressing his feeling as is the raising of the hat as a mark of respect today. It is conventional to raise the hat and uncover the head in the presence of death today, and yet it is a truthful expression of an emotion which is really and sincerely felt; and this was equally true of wringing of another's hand; it was conventional and yet a truthful expression of emotion really and sincerely felt in Shakespeare's day.

Interestingly enough, in his painting of the incident, Poussin shows Coriolanus wringing the hand of Volumnia in the very way described by Bulwer; and the same thing is shown in Hayman's illustration (based on Poussin) in Hanmer's edition of Shakespeare in 1746. Of course, this is no proof that the same business was used in the eighteenth-century performances; nor could it ever be more than the most indirect evidence that Shakespeare's own actor did what Bulwer describes. But we can be sure that whatever that actor did, he did it because it was demanded from him by what he felt in the situation which Shakespeare had imagined. If Bulwer's gesture was used, its use sprang from no arbitrary or external symbolic value, but from the fact that it allowed him to express what he had to.

For the modern actor the lesson of this seems to me that if he were to find that by wringing Volumnia's hand as described by Bulwer he was expressing what he felt, then what he felt would at once be obvious to his audience, who would neither be puzzled by his action, nor preen itself on recognizing an esoteric and archaic gesture used unscrupulously as a gimmick. Any actor who really and truthfully expresses his emotion in this gesture will give his audience no opportunity to do anything but feel with him. But if he cannot feel really and truthfully when performing this 'action', he must obviously find his own way of expressing the emotions which have not yet been put into words as he confronts his mother before he speaks those which Shakespeare has then given him. And then, whatever he does will be right if he has no alternative but to do it as Coriolanus in this situation.

Although we have very little evidence about Elizabethan stage-playing as such, what there is leaves no doubt that Shakespeare's contemporaries demanded from their actors the truthful expression of real emotion and the identification of the player with the character whom he represented. In each of these respects rhetorical acting remained true to its source and inspiration. The rhetoricians placed in the forefront of their art the truthful expression in action of genuinely felt emotion; and, as we have seen in an earlier chapter, they insisted that whenever a school text required the speaker to be identified with the person whose words he was speaking, the boys were to pronounce 'as if they themselves were the persons that did speak in that dialogue.' (See pp. 13 ff.)

Elizabethan stage-playing was essentially a matter of expressing externally in a truthful manner what was felt really and truthfully within. In Hamlet's account of the Player's reaction when speaking the lines concerned with the agony of the 'mobled queen' we are told what happened externally as the expression of a deeply felt emotion within. From the working of his soul

> all his visage wann'd;
> Tears in his eyes, distraction in's aspect,
> A broken voice, and his whole function suiting
> With forms to his conceit.
>
> (II, ii, 547–50)

And in their action, too, the rhetoricians insisted in theory and showed in practice that a speaker's 'whole function' ought to suit 'with forms' to what he was expressing from

ACTION AND THE WORD

within. The Player's face went pale because he really felt horror; it was because he felt distracted that distraction showed 'in's aspect'; the grief which he really felt gave him 'a broken voice', this did not derive from any system of external conventions. The rhetorician, too, relied upon genuinely felt emotion, however hard he had worked like the actor at acquiring the technique of expressing it; everybody agreed that it was 'almost impossible for an orator to stir up a passion in his auditors, except he be first affected with the same passion himself.'[1] The right way was not to use gesture externally as an end in itself, but to feel the emotion within and to let it express itself in what was seen and heard in the delivery without. Whatever the orator might do with his hands, face, eyes, body and posture was not the result of studying a conventional system of gesture to be applied from without, but came from the need to express in action a truly and deeply felt emotion. What Hamlet says of the Player is given us in prose, but in words that are by no means prosaic, by Thomas Wright:

> as the internal affection is more vehement, so the external persuasion will be more potent: for the passion in the persuader seemeth to me to resemble the wind a trumpeter bloweth in at one end of the trumpet, and in what manner it proceedeth from him, so it issueth forth at the other end, and cometh to our ears; even so the passion proceedeth from the heart, and is blown about the body, face, eyes, hands, voice, and so by gestures passeth into our eyes, and by sounds into our ears.[2]

This again is an account of 'the whole function suiting with forms' to the emotion experienced within. As the orator's passion proceeds from the heart and 'is blown about the body, face, eyes, hands, voice', it expressed itself in his

[1]Wright, *op. cit.*, p. 172.
[2]*Ibid.*, p. 174.

90

external action in such ways as we find treated and illustrated by Bulwer. His *Chirologia* and *Chironomia* deal with the part played by arm, hand and fingers in that 'external action' which was so well described as a 'shadow of affections', that is, an image of emotions.

There is no need to be afraid that the rhetoricians will lead us astray in our search for information on the expressing of emotion in stage-playing. They knew that they could not hope to be effective, either as orators in particular or as users of language in general, unless they mastered the art of imaging in delivery the emotion expressed in their words, which had to be felt within as they spoke them. Knowing, and giving due weight to this knowledge, that action was an externalizing of what was within, the rhetoricians looked upon the stage-players as models who constantly showed this very process taking place freely, sincerely, and truthfully, without constraint, yet with that smoothness and control which belong to art. For the orator no less than for the actor, action was 'an external image of an internal mind, or a shadow of affections, or three springs which flow from one fountain, called *vox, vultus, vita*, voice, countenance, life'. It was described as 'universally . . . a natural or artificial moderation, qualification, modification or composition of the voice, countenance, and gesture of the body, proceeding from some passion, and apt to stir up the like'.[1] And Wright, whose words these are, declares that to do this the orator should notice how men and women behave in real life under the stress of emotion; then he should 'leave the excess and exorbitant levity or other defects, and keep the manner corrected with a prudent mediocrity'. ('You must acquire and beget', says Hamlet, 'a temperance that may give it smoothness.') If our orator wanted a model, nowhere would he find a better example of the heightening of nature into art than in the play-houses: 'this the best may be marked in stage-players', says Wright, 'who act excel-

[1] T. Wright, *op. cit.*, p. 176.

91

lently, for as the perfection of their exercise consisteth in imitation of others, so they that imitate best act best.'[1]

Elizabethan actors acted and imitated so well because their art was based on identification. Hamlet's Player is completely identified and lives imaginatively a witness of the terrible scenes at the sack of Troy. At the same time, as his whole function suits with forms to his conceit, what he actually conceives does not remain intellectualized, but is experienced as something which is happening to himself, not to an eyewitness giving a description as imagined by a poet. The Player's own emotions are evoked; they are what he expresses because he is able to 'force his soul so to his own conceit' that what he had imagined intellectually of the fall of Troy has now become felt as his own experience. The few statements which exist about the art of stage-playing show that there was nothing unusual in the firm identification of Hamlet's Player. Heywood enthuses that when an actor plays a heroic part, the audience reacts to him 'as if the personator were the man personated'.[2] Hopton talks of actors who 'appear to you to be the self-same men' as they impersonate.[3] And the Character of *An Excellent Actor* declares 'what we see him personate we think truly done before us'.[4] Just after the Restoration, moreover, speaking of Burbage, Flecknoe tells us that actor 'was a delightful Proteus, so wholly transforming himself into his part, and putting off himself with his clothes, as he never (not so much as in the tiring-house) assumed himself again until the play was done'.[5]

In the training of rhetoricians, we remember, identification was equally important. Part of this training involved speaking in character 'where persons or things are feigned

[1] *Ibid.*, p. 179.
[2] T. Heywood, *An Apology for Actors* (1612), sig. B4[r].
[3] A. Hopton, Commendatory Poem in Heywood's *Apology*, sig. a I[v].
[4] *New and Choice Characters* (1615), ed. F. L. Lucas, *The Works of John Webster* (1927), IV, 42.
[5] R. Flecknoe, *A Short Discourse of the English Stage* (1664), ed. Spingarn, *Critical Essays of the Seventeenth Century* (1908), II, 95.

to speak'; and boys at school were to be made to 'utter every dialogue lively . . . and so in every other speech, to imagine themselves to have occasion to utter the very same things'. The exercises in pronouncing 'passionate figures', those which expressed emotion, also entailed a forcing of the soul to the speaker's conceit, so that he might really feel the emotion which was to make its way outward to expression in 'external action'. We need not fear that the rhetoricians of the renaissance are likely to lead us away from what is vital to real acting today, that is, away from the insistence that the actor must be identified with his role, and that emotion must be experienced within before there is any possibility of moving others by external acting.

Of course, there is an essential difference between the actor and the orator; yet this does not prevent their sharing the same principles and the same practice when it is a matter of external action. The orator speaks in his own person; he does not have to imagine that he is somebody imaginary, he does not have to use his own truthfully felt emotion to represent the imaginary person he is playing as if he were the very man. But the actor must. As Wright puts it, 'onely they differ in this, that these act feignedly' while 'those act really'.[1] Nevertheless in each the body, face, and voice express a truthfully felt emotion from within. It is true that the actor expresses his emotion in the person of another, while the orator expresses his emotion in his own person; yet in each case the emotion is truly felt, and in each case expression is through external action. And when it comes to using *vox, vultus, vita*, voice, face, movement, to externalize the emotion, what applies in principle to the Elizabethan actor applied equally to the orator; as for their practice, we have Wright's word that 'in the substance of external action for most part orators and stage-players agree'.[2] This means that writers like Bulwer can be

[1] T. Wright, *op. cit.*, p. 179.
[2] *Ibid.*

taken as a guide to that 'most part' of action in which there was agreement. Their descriptions of individual gesture— what Wright calls the 'minching details'—treat those things in which the rhetoricians were content to conform to the example of the players. But it was felt that some things were not fitting to orators even though they were practised by the players; these things we cannot expect to find in accounts of rhetorical action, except when a writer such as Bulwer or Fraunce is at pains to tell his reader exactly what stage practices to avoid.

The relation between acting and oratory in renaissance England is sometimes incorrectly assumed to be one in which the actor adopted and transcended rhetorical techniques, turning them into something else. But in reality the actors did to perfection what the orators were also striving after; it was the orators who used the techniques of the actors and not vice versa. And it is for this very reason that renaissance accounts of rhetorical techniques are valuable sources for a knowledge of Elizabethan stage-playing. For we have in them details of what rhetoricians shared with the stage. And knowing this it now becomes clear why the Character of *An Excellent Actor* declares: 'Whatsoever is commendable in the grave orator is most exquisitely perfect in him, for by a full and significant action of body he charms our attention.'[1]

Actor and orator both work with a 'full and significant action of body' to express their emotion and to embody their words in Shakespeare's England. But as we should expect, the actor was the better of the two. Where the orator's action was good enough to be found 'commendable', it was still quite outshone by what was in the actor an exquisite perfection. For the actor was more practised, apart from questions of respective aptitudes; his whole art was 'action'; he devoted his whole professional life to it—and for actors the professional life is often very nearly the whole of life.

[1] Ed. Lucas, IV, 42.

Not only were the actors more practised in the minutiae of external technique so that body and voice responded more perfectly to thought and emotion, but they were better both at feeling emotion and at identifying themselves with the characters they were playing.

On these fundamental points we are at one today with both Elizabethan orators and actors. Rhetorical treatises have nothing to tell us about how to learn to feel emotion where it is needed, or how to identify ourselves with a character; but fortunately we know enough in these directions and do not need Elizabethan help. Where the Elizabethans can help us, however, is in the task of expressing emotion truthfully and identifying oneself, when the emotion and character are created in an Elizabethan dramatic text, and have to be represented bodily in terms of the formality or comparative formality of that text. For while naturalistic acting inevitably clashes with the style of the Elizabethan unrealistic text and thus falsifies and distorts, its core of truthfully felt and truthfully expressed emotion orientated towards an objective is still no less essential to the satisfactory acting of an Elizabethan play.

Flecknoe's praise of Burbage points out to us our way. Burbage had 'all the parts of an excellent orator',[1] and through them he created the roles in which he was so strongly identified. In this creation of the whole character the parts were transcended. The parts shared with excellent orators were used as they ought to be used to represent an imaginary person as if he had really come to life. And among these parts were the techniques of trained voice, countenance and body, the ability to read the text with an awareness of its structure as well as its meaning, both as literature and as the expression of the wishes, emotions, intentions of an imagined character: then in acting the role, voice, face and body became the external image of all that was imagined and actually felt. Once the mind and

[1] *Op. cit.*, p. 95.

body had been trained it was left to the wind of which Wright speaks to blow through them, making them trumpet-tongued, as the inner feeling had its way with the instrument.

A 'full and significant action' not only represented emotion, it also embodied the literature as such: 'For action', says Wright, 'is either a certain visible eloquence, or an eloquence of the body, or a comely grace in delivering conceits.'[1] The Elizabethan actor's style was decided fundamentally by that of his words, and this ought to be true of the acting of Shakespeare today. The degree of realism is determined by the words. That is what Sir Richard Baker was saying with his determined insistence that the pleasure of a play acted by Alleyn or Burbage lay in 'the ingeniousness of the speech when it is fitted to the person'; the speech, for all that it is an artifact and pretends to be nothing else, expresses truthfully the nature of its speaker. It is ingenious and not nature, but it expresses nature. But pleasure, said Baker, lay also in 'the gracefulness of the action when it is fitted to the speech'. The acting gives pleasure because it is graceful, because it is art; but it is art which like the speech expresses the nature of the character as that has been created by the dramatist in his medium of words.

Baker is talking only of the sources of the pleasure which we get from watching a play, he is not talking about the nature of that pleasure itself. He is certainly not attempting to distinguish philosophically between the nature of a play acted and that of a play read, when he says that in performance there is more pleasure to be derived than in reading. He is talking empirically, remarking on what everybody knows from experience, that a reader is denied the pleasure given to a spectator by the quality of an actor's movements, the 'gracefulness of the action'. But Baker does not say by any means that only in acting are the potentialities of a speech made actual; he says merely that performance gives

[1] *Op. cit.*, p. 176.

Josephine Wilson as Lady Macbeth.

*'Nought's had, all's spent, where our desire is got
without content.'*

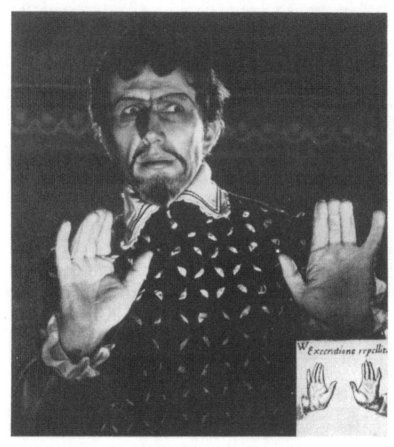

Bernard Miles as Macbeth.

'Who should against his murderer shut the door.'

Bernard Miles as Macbeth.

'The swift, the slow, the subtle, the housekeeper, the hunter . . .'

'My husband lives that Tybalt would have slain . . .

And Tybalt's dead that would have slain my husband . . .

All this is comfort.'

Elizabeth Shepherd as Juliet.

an extra pleasure which comes from hearing and watching the actor. Reading to ourselves we may have the same impression of the character, the same apprehension of the actual play, but we miss the pleasure of an actor's voice and movement. Baker is therefore not contradicting himself when he insists that a player only says 'that without book, which we may read within book'. He can still declare that there is greater pleasure to be derived when the player acts: 'And we may well acknowledge that gracefulness of action is the greatest pleasure of a play, seeing it is the greatest pleasure of the art of pleasure, rhetoric.'[1] Just as the greatest pleasure given by an orator comes from seeing and hearing him, so the player's action likewise gives the greatest pleasure of a play.

Both orator and actor in Shakespeare's day expressed sincerely felt emotion in details of voice, countenance and gesture which truthfully imaged it, and which truthfully embodied the lines as literature. The gracefulness of their action fitted the speech, and that in its turn already fitted the person. This was full and significant action. And just as the orator took the actor for his model, so we today can learn from what is preserved of the actor's art in the treatises on rhetorical delivery. Our task is to act in a manner which suits the Elizabethan text (in which speech is fitted to person), the modern actor and the modern audience. And after the basic principles are clear there is much to be gained from considering the actual details of Elizabethan gesture; but we must never forget that no attempt should be made to impose Elizabethan details on a modern acting style suited to modern plays, which demands from the actor an attitude of mind and emotion quite unsuited to Shakespeare.

The gestures of the hand and arm discussed and illustrated by John Bulwer belong among the parts of an excellent orator which the rhetoricians took over from the

[1]Sir Richard Baker, *Theatrum Triumphans* (1670), pp. 34; 43.

actors. The more we become familiar with them, the more doubtful does it become whether they ought to be described specifically as 'renaissance' gestures, if by the use of the word 'renaissance' it is implied that they are not used or even not known today. One, for instance, is called by Bulwer *floccifaccit*; he describes it thus: 'The middle finger strongly compressed by the thumb, and their collision producing a flurting sound, and the hand so cast out, is an action convenient to slight and undervalue, and to express the vanity of things.'[1] But as Bernard Miles has observed to the present writer, this is not an obsolete, specifically 'renaissance' gesture: 'Victure Mature snapped his fingers at me only five days ago in just the sense of your gesture.'[2] Yet during rehearsals for the production of *Macbeth* at the Mermaid Theatre in St. John's Wood some years earlier, in 1952, this gesture seemed too esoteric to Geoffrey Taylor, who preferred not to use it, when, as Malcolm, he gave an account of the dignity and impressiveness of Cawdor's behaviour as he met his death on the scaffold. Here, however, the actor found himself changing his mind after playing the role for some nights; and to our mutual delight he quite spontaneously expressed in the gesture his sense of Cawdor's quality

> As one that had been studied in his death
> To throw away the dearest thing he ow'd
> As 'twere a careless trifle.
>
> (I, iv, 9–11)

In the same production Lady Macbeth's contempt for her husband expressed itself in the same 'action convenient to slight and undervalue' as she hissed at him

> From this time
> Such I account thy love.
>
> (I, vii, 38–39)

[1]*Chiron.*, p. 81. See also *Chirol.*, p. 176.
[2]In a letter dated 5 February 1956.

And here the action is required to make the meaning of the words really clear.

A year earlier when an experimental production of the first scene of *Hamlet* gave me a first opportunity to try to develop an acting style for Shakespeare with a professional cast, Marcellus was asked if he would accompany his series of questions to Bernardo and Horatio with a slight turn and lift of the hand. For Bulwer says that while the hand cannot be used to ask a question, 'yet commonly when we demand, however it be composed, we use to change or turn our hand, raising it a little upwards.'[1] The actor did this as he spoke the passage beginning

> Why this same strict and most observant watch
> So nightly toils the subject of the land;
>
> (I, 1, 71–79)

Here again, had it not been for this passage in Bulwer the actor would not have asked the questions in this way; and yet the gesture is not by any means obsolete or unknown today. 'I've always turned up my hands to give a questioning,' writes Bernard Miles, '—so have all actors.'[2] But while the actors often do these things, there is no longer a tradition of doing them spontaneously when acting Shakespeare on those many occasions when they could express for the actor very powerfully and satisfactorily what he is feeling and wanting in the person of the imagined character.

The experiments in the Mermaid seasons of 1951–3 were in very many ways imperfect; yet little as any of us would be prepared to claim for them as artistic successes, these productions established the certainty that so-called 'renaissance' or 'rhetorical' gesture allows modern actors to externalize truthfully and adequately the emotion they are feeling; and the result shows itself not only in the actor's increased satisfaction in what he is doing, but in what fol-

[1]*Chiron*, p. 37.
[2]In a letter to the author, dated 5 February 1956.

lows then as a matter of course; the audience has a clearer and greater sense of what is going on, and the words have greater effect. We also found that by acquiring some understanding of the relation between the gesture, the text, and the emotions felt by the actor, individual players became aware of ways of evolving movement which satisfied them and which suited Shakespeare's words quite independent of any tradition of gesture in the past.

Bulwer makes a rough and ready distinction between two different ways in which the action can be suited to the word. In *Chirologia* he concentrates on the externalizing of emotion; but *Chironomia* deals more especially with gesture which enforces meaning and which lends itself to making the listener respond to, even if not consciously aware of, the structure and development of a speech or of an argument. In actual fact no hard and fast distinction can be made between these two aspects of gesture, they blend into one another; for instance, *Chironomia* includes an account of the movement in which the hand 'propellant to the leftward' suits a negative; and however much one may argue that this is a 'regulated accessory' of what Bulwer calls the 'fair-spoken adjuncts of rhetorical utterance',[1] it is also an expression of the emotion which insists on the sweeping away of a repellent idea or suggestion.

At the Mermaid in its early years we found help in much that was said by Bulwer on the externalizing of emotion. 'To wring the hands', he tells us,' is a natural expression of excessive grief, used by those who condole, bewail and lament.' This interlacing of the fingers and pressing together of the palms expresses the effect of that pressure of grief on the brain which Francis Bacon declared to be the mechanical cause of tears.[2] Lady Macbeth wrung her hands in this way as she considered the dangers into which she and her husband had run, in her case all unwittingly (III, ii,

[1]*Chiron.*, p. 43. See also pp. 52 f. and *Chirol.*, p. 54.
[2]*Chirol.*, p. 28.

100

4–7), and the same 'weeping cross' helped to express Lady Macduff's emotion as she asked bitterly, 'Why, then, alas! Do I put up that womanly defence?' (IV, ii, 76–77). Although the gesture is associated with grief it is essentially a miming of the act of pressing moisture out, and therefore seemed suitable for the witch who rejoices malevolently, 'I'll drain him dry as hay.' (I, iii, 18.) The gesture is effective in this case because the emotion flows out so strongly as the witch feels herself wringing the hated shipman dry, draining him of vitality between her very fingers.

Another gesture which would have been used effectively by many an actor until well into the nineteenth century is described by Bulwer in the following words: 'Both hands objected with the palms adverse, is a foreright adjunct of pronunciation, fit to help the utterance of words coming out in detestation, despite and exprobration.'[1] Because he was not applying the gesture externally but feeling Macbeth's emotion from inside, Bernard Miles was able to express that emotion sincerely and effectively, as he asserted that Duncan's host should 'against his murderer shut the door'. (I, vii, 15. See illustrations.)

Bulwer relates that when Sir Francis Bacon made a report on duelling to the Star Chamber ('being then His Majesty's Attorney General'), he denounced 'the hot spirited gallants of those times' who claimed that as the law offered them no protection for their honour they were forced to resort to the sword to defend themselves from what they considered 'a mortal wound to the reputation' conveyed by an insulting gesture known as the 'fillip'. Bulwer speaks of this gesture as a 'trivial expression whereby we with a fillip inflict a trifling punishment, or a scoff'. He describes it as 'to bend the middle finger while it stiffly resteth upon the thumb, and so in jesting-wise to let it off'.[2]

The engraved title of *Chironomia* shows the fillip being

[1] *Chiron.*, p. 54.
[2] *Chirol.*, pp. 177 f.

administered by an amiable enough personage in hood and furred gown who is labelled Cicero; but comparatively harmless as it might appear to modern eyes, it was said of it in the seventeenth century, 'this slighting expression of the fingers gives such a slur of disgrace if used to men, that it hath been thought such a disparagement as wounded a tender reputation'.[1] In the Mermaid productions of *Macbeth*, Young Siward accompanied his words with this 'fillip' when, confronting Macbeth within the castle, he cried, 'Thou liest, abhorred tyrant.' Macbeth was stung immediately by the insult, while Siward drew back his hand to grasp his sword, adding:

> with my sword
> I'll prove the lie thou speakest.
>
> (v, vii, 10–11)

In Bulwer's illustration the gesture seems harmless, even ludicrous; but it can easily be charged with malice and contempt, creating tense excitement as it flicks insult on the stage. It is an admirable way for Tybalt to add to the insult of his words to Romeo. The 'fillip' can also be used in a less insulting manner, as an accompaniment, for instance, to Celia's desire to sit and 'mock the good housewife Fortune from her wheel'. (i, ii, 28–29.) In the Mermaid production of *As You Like It* at the Royal Exchange in 1953 our Celia imagined herself both mocking at and flicking Fortune from her wheel.

The examples which have just been considered are typical of the gesture expressing emotion in that they are self-explanatory and can be understood immediately without any initiation into a code; and this is especially true when they accompany words. The other type of gesture is also self-explanatory to some extent; but even when it is not, if it accompanies words it presents no difficulty whatsoever to the onlooker. Bulwer tells us 'the two inferior fingers shut

---

[1] *Ibid.*, p. 178.

in, and the other three presented in an eminent posture in the extended hand, is a speaking action, significant to demand silence, and procure audience'.[1] This was used with literally awe-inspiring effect, by Bernard Miles as the Ghost in the first scene of *Hamlet* at St. John's Wood in 1951. As Horatio begged the spirit for the fourth time to speak, Mr. Miles lifted his head (till then he had been gazing downward) and stretched up his arm and hand with the fingers as described by Bulwer. We actually saw what Horatio speaks of later to Hamlet, when he says that the Ghost

> did address
> Itself to motion, like as it would speak.
>
> (I, ii, 216–17)

Having held the attention of the audience with what according to Bulwer is 'motion, like as it would speak', the Ghost's hand dropped to its left side and then started to go out as if to accompany words which were about to be spoken, the mouth starting to open as if to speak them. At that moment came the cock-crow; the expected words were never uttered; the splendid commanding figure shrank into a furtive, even evil-looking, shape; it 'started like a guilty thing' and was gone.

Bernard Miles made equally effective and equally truthful use of another of these gestures of the second type in the two productions of *Macbeth*. 'The right index,' says Bulwer, 'if it marshal-like go from finger to finger, to note them with a light touch, it doth fit their purpose who would number their arguments, and by a visible distinction set them all on a row upon their fingers.'[2] This Macbeth did not number his arguments, but he enumerated on his fingers the different kinds of dogs in his mind as he taunted the murderers and reminded them that the valued file distinguishes

---

[1] *Chiron.*, p. 67.
[2] *Ibid.*, p. 83.

> the swift, the slow, the subtle,
> The house-keeper, the hunter.

(III, i, 95–96)

It is relevant to point out that one critic wrote that 'retrospective analysis' could 'identify the finger count, *the swift, the slow, the subtle*, etc., as a rhetorical figure, but at the time one was primarily aware of the dramatic effect'.[1]

It had been the dramatic effect which was dominant a year earlier when Bernardo's indignation that Horatio should refuse to credit a dreaded sight 'twice seen of us' expressed itself in two fingers of the right hand struck forcibly against the palm of the left. From one point of view this might be criticized as a questionable device to make the audience see 'two' as it heard the word spoken; but the justification for the movement comes from its allowing Bernardo to express that he is feeling indignation because he is sure that he has seen it not once, but twice. And of course his voice and his look, indeed his body as a whole, expressed the same indignation.

One of the difficulties of Horatio's account of the long feud of Denmark with Norway in this same scene comes from the fact that he is speaking about three persons, Fortinbras the elder, Hamlet the elder and young Fortinbras. In the first part of the speech he has to keep the elder Fortinbras and the elder Hamlet apart in his mind, and in the minds of those who are listening to him, whether these are Bernardo and Marcellus on the stage with him, or his audience off it in the auditorium. In 1951 we found that the actor helped both himself and his listeners when he did what is described by Bulwer as suitable to an antithesis: 'If both hands by turns behave themselves with equal art, they fitly move to set off any matter that goes by way of antithesis or opposition.'[2] And so whenever Horatio referred to the dead

[1]Roy Walker, *Theatre* (1952), VII, No. 156, p. 12.
[2]*Chiron.*, p. 58.

Hamlet he let his right hand allude to the person he was distinguishing in his mind, while the left hand did the same for old Fortinbras. And when he came to 'Now, sir, young Fortinbras,' his voice and body reflected the effort he was making to be sure that he would not be misunderstood as still speaking about the elder of that name: and the point was driven home by his right hand, with its first finger making a slight yet definite gesture (as if to say 'this one, not the other') as the word 'young' was spoken. The same principle of setting off 'fitly' a matter 'that goes by way of antithesis' was applied in an amateur production of *Romeo and Juliet* in the University of Bristol, with, so far as one could ascertain, quite satisfactory results. Juliet, suddenly realizing that what matters most in life to her is her husband's safety, spoke 'My husband lives that Tybalt would have slain', with her right hand and arm extended half to the front and half sideways, as if placing on the hand her realization of the fact that the man who matters to her has not been killed by Tybalt. Then the same thing happened with her left hand and arm as she spoke 'And Tybalt's dead that would have slain my husband.' And this time she was grasping the reality that the man who has been killed wanted to kill her husband. With both arms spread wide, she gathered up to herself a complete awareness of the consolation that all that matters is Romeo, and that Romeo lives, bringing her hands together, expressing gratitude for the knowledge in clasping them, before the next thought strikes, 'Wherefore weep I then?' (III, ii, 105–7.) (See illustrations.)

As I have been at pains to insist, ideally gesture must come from within. Nevertheless there are times when the purely external application of a cliché in preparing a role can initiate the chain-reaction which will release an actor from whatever has been inhibiting from feeling truthfully and deeply. Stanislavski gives an example of this happening in his account of Tortsov starting with a purely external cliché which released in him the inner feeling required. It was 'an undoubted fact that his inner faculties responded to the external image he had created, and adjusted to it'.[1] Similarly some of the obvious external signs of emotion can be used as a starting-point by the modern actor. Bulwer tells us, what we all know, that a clenched fist is a sign of rage; anyone who invariably expressed rage in a role by means of this external cliché would excite the derision he deserved; yet in preparing a role the actor might easily find that instead of being a substitute for rage, his clenching his fist might help him to start on the course of developing the feeling and then the complete expression of real rage, which might not otherwise have been attained. Stanislavski goes even farther and relates how, by starting with a conventional trait traditionally attached to a typical member of a foreign nation, 'Tortsov vividly demonstrated that external characterization can be achieved intuitively and also by means of a purely technical, mechanical, simple external trick.'[2]

Sometimes when an actor cannot infuse into his voice the quality of his inner experience, a purely external gesture or movement may enable him to do so. For instance, when Macbeth says, 'If it were done, when 'tis done,' the first 'done' means 'done with once and for all'. In preparation of the role the actor may find himself aided in the task of distinguishing between the first 'done' and the second (which means merely 'performed') by using his hands in a swift sharp movement of negation to express his desire to annihilate all possibility of repercussion. Or he may find one hand alone sufficient to express this need of the character's. In some such way he will find that the full quality of what he is trying to express will now come into his voice; and once it is there he can almost certainly retain it without the gesture, unless he finds himself needing that, too.

[1] *Building a Character* (1950), p. 9.
[2] *Ibid.*

But the same release from inhibition can be obtained by a movement which does not fit the implication of the words, though it may express their surface sense. For instance I have known an actor who could not express the sense and feeling of change in his voice when speaking the word 'turn' in Capulet's

> All things that we ordained festival
> Turn from their office to black funeral.
>
> (IV, v, 84–85)

But the meaning came into his voice on this word when he merely imagined himself spreading his hand round a small wheel and turning it clock-wise as he grasped it. Once he was able to make his inner faculties respond by means of this movement, he found he could dispense with it.

Of course some actors are able to express all that they need in the voice without the help of movement. When John Glen played Banquo at the Mermaid in 1952 he was not helped at all by the suggestion that he might make use of the hand gesture which is 'convenient to slight and undervalue' (see pp. 98 f.) as he warned Macbeth that the instruments of darkness, 'Win us with honest trifles'. (I, iii, 125.) He was able to express in his voice alone the contradiction of 'honest' and 'trifles', emphasizing the worthlessness of what was honest here. But another actor might well have found the gesture a great help, and have continued to use it in performance, simply because it enabled him to image all the more completely all that he was feeling and trying to do in the person of Banquo.

What Stanislavski has to say of the fluent movements and poses ('attitudes' as they were once called in England) belonging to the conventional acting of his day, as resembling ballet, is applicable to the use of 'countenance and body' in the acting of Shakespeare. Theatrical gestures are of no use when they move along 'an external superficial line'. But these stage conventions can be adapted in order to carry out 'some vital purpose, the projection of some inner experience'. Then, as he says, the gesture becomes transcended into 'real action with purpose and content'.[1] But in the change it does not lose its fluency or its grace. Indeed, grace of movement should not be neglected even in 'the very torrent, tempest, and, as I may say, whirlwind of your passion'; though, of course, it should not be allowed to become the first consideration and so degenerate into affectation.

A study of the principles of 'renaissance' rhetorical delivery and of the actual details of gesture in a writer like Bulwer can most definitely help many modern actors in their problem of acting Shakespeare. Not only can we adapt or use gestures actually described in the past, but we can learn from them how to evolve our own, as in the following example. Bernard Miles entered as Macbeth in the second scene of Act Three in 1952 and 1953 with the crossed arms or wreathed arms which were for the Elizabethans a typical sign of brooding and melancholy. And when Lady Macbeth had asked him why he brooded alone and admonished him to forget what he had done, or not to brood on it, he replied at first with his arms still folded. But when he came to the words 'let the frame of things disjoint, both the worlds suffer', he attained his inner reality and externalized it in a breaking apart of the knot of his arms, while his two clenched fists, falling slowly and as though with effort (yet still gracefully) to his sides, completed the full imaging of the selfish determination to triumph at no matter what cost to others. Part of this movement, the breaking apart of the wreathed arms and the two pounding fists, was not derived from Elizabethan tradition, but came from the wind of passion blowing through the trumpet of the actor. Nevertheless the passion was released and realized by the typical gesture of crossed arms, the 'token' of melancholy. And we have here a perfect example of what Stanislavski was saying

[1] *Op. cit.*, p. 49.

108

when he reminded actors that 'the typical gesture' helps to bring a player 'closer to the character he is portraying, while the intrusion of personal motions separates him from it and pushes him in the direction of his personal emotions'.[1]

The aim, of course, is to use his personal emotions in order to portray those of the character. And when an actor has to play with truth and reality the real emotions expressed by an unrealistic Elizabethan text, he may often find that his difficulties may be overcome by taking the kind of advantage of what there is to learn from the Elizabethans which I have suggested in this chapter. Whatever the actor does must suit him personally; but it must also suit the author's text, and it must be real and truthful for the audience.

[1]*Op. cit.*, p. 76.

Five

CHARACTER

THEORETICALLY there are two processes involved in the preparation of a role; they are not really distinct in practice, of course, but it is useful to consider them separately in order to see some of the problems of creating character more clearly. One of these processes is a matter of attaining an intellectual knowledge of what the words mean and why the character has to use them; in this way we find out the emotion expressed in them and the character's objective. This process is shared with students of Shakespeare who are not actors; but the other process referred to is one which the actor does not share with academic students of Shakespeare, who are usually content with a merely intellectual knowledge. The actor, however, has to progress to a point at which he feels in himself sincerely as his own emotion what he knows intellectually the imaginary character has been imagined as feeling. It is not a matter of seeming to feel the emotions, but of really feeling them; then he can seem to be the character. But all the time that he seems to be the very character come to life he is in fact really feeling the emotions expressed in the character's words, and really wanting to attain the character's objective. Every actor blends these two processes in the way which suits his individuality.

Here I have very little to say about the second of these two processes; and that little is best said after we have considered the other, the process whereby an actor comes to know intellectually what it is he must feel and want before he can speak his lines as if there is nothing else possible for him to do when playing the character on the stage. This book is not about how to act, but about some of the ways in which it is possible to prepare to act a Shakespearian role; acting is the same whether we act Shakespeare or John Osborne; but to prepare to act Shakespeare is a different matter from preparing to act John Osborne, because Shakespeare requires a different effort from us if we are to know intellectually what is to be felt, and what is the character's objective. Words have changed their sense and their implications, and the real emotion and desires have been expressed unrealistically. For that reason a modern actor finds it harder to be certain exactly what it is Shakespeare's words need him to feel and want if he is to speak them as one having no alternative but to speak them and in that way. It is with the attaining of the intellectual certainty (without insisting that it always can be attained) that I am concerned here. For when it has been found it gives a confidence and satisfaction both to the actor and his audience which cannot be produced any other way.

The earlier chapters of this book have been concerned with seeing intellectually the relation of arrangements of words and of the structure of the lines to the surface sense, its implications, the emotions and objectives. It has also been suggested that when this vision has been acquired the actor finds himself speaking the verse or prose in the way which is right both for it and for him; his voice gives the music which the lines ought to evoke from it and from his personality; and his audience is given more complete understanding of what is being spoken and acted, not because he is striving deliberately to make them hear the contrast between one word and another in the poet's pattern, but because the absorbing of the text which allows him to feel the emotion and want the objective expressed in the pattern, also allows him to make the pattern 'manifest' to his audience. It would be truer to say that there is no alternative but to make the pattern manifest, but not because he is trying to. His success comes as an inevitable by-product of his confidence, his understanding of how everything works together to enable him to play the role to the satisfaction of his own conscience as an artist. That is what really matters to him; it is a lucky audience that hears him when his artistic conscience really is satisfied.

Clear and careful examination of the surface sense and the structure of the text is the first step to achieving the satisfaction of which we are thinking. And a good illustration of how precise reading leads to rich and satisfying portrayal of character can be found in the speech in which Othello likens his 'bloody thoughts' to the flow of water from the Black Sea through the Sea of Marmora to the Dardanelles (III, iii, 457–464). The speech falls naturally into two parts, in the first of which there is concentration on the idea of a current running on without an indication of the slightest possibility that anything else could happen. The current is icy, but it does not freeze and become motionless; it runs on for ever in its compelled and compelling course.

> Like to the Pontic sea,
> Whose icy current and compulsive course
> Ne'er feels retiring ebb, but keeps due on
> To the Propontic and the Hellespont.

In the second half of the speech, Othello lets us know that what he has really had in mind when concentrating on the undeviating current is the implacability of his 'bloody thoughts'.

> Even so my bloody thoughts, with violent pace,
> Shall ne'er look back, ne'er ebb to humble love,

112

Till that a capable and wide revenge
Swallow them up.

Some of the details of the second half of the simile are the
equivalents of details in the first: the bloody thoughts are
like the Pontic sea; 'ne'er feels retiring ebb' has as its
counterpart 'ne'er ebb to humble love', and the equivalent
of 'but keeps due on' is 'shall ne'er look back'. But the
correspondence between the two halves of the simile is not
exact. While the progress of the Pontic sea goes no farther
than the Hellespont, that of the bloody thoughts goes on
into what is the equivalent of the Mediterranean, which is
not even mentioned explicitly. These thoughts must drive
on until they enter something large enough to absorb their
current—'Till that a capable and wide revenge/Swallow
them up.' Careful comparison of the two halves makes us see
that in fact the narrowness of the channel for the Pontic
sea makes depth no brake on its movement; and similarly
it is useless for Othello to have anything less than a comprehensive and 'wide' revenge if his resentment is to be
swallowed up. He is not yearning for a deep revenge; the
word 'wide' is used precisely; it is the word which Othello
must use to express his need. The same need is expressed in
the word 'capable', which in Shakespeare's time had the
sense 'comprehensive'. Othello does not know how many
people are involved, not in the enjoyment of Desdemona's
favours, but in making a fool of him, in making use of him
for the good of the Venetian state, in concealing from him
the truth about Desdemona, and letting him think he was
being encouraged in the love of a splendid woman, when all
the time there was really a sort of unspoken conspiracy to
use him. It is from this that his resentment springs; and the
resentment wants vengeance on all, however many they
are, who have made a fool of him. In this sense of isolation,
only Iago seems a true friend; everyone else is the potential
object of Othello's bloody thoughts; they will be assuaged by

nothing less than all-inclusive and utter revenge on everyone who can be shown to have been involved in the conspiracy against him.

Examination of the surface sense leads to other important implications for the person who is preparing to act Othello. The emotive 'feels' does not really apply to the Pontic sea but to the resolution to have nothing less than a 'capable and wide revenge', which itself can only be expressed in the image of the sea. 'Retiring ebb' in the first half of the simile is not rendered exactly by 'look back' in the second; the exact equivalent here is 'turn back' or 'draw back'. Yet the word 'look' is not used loosely; if his thoughts were directed away from the imagined vengeance, back to the image of his past love for Desdemona, they and he would be softened; they literally must not look back. There is equal precision in the choice of the word humble in 'ne'er ebb to humble love'. To look back would mean to turn back, to ebb; instead of sweeping on to their goal in outraged pride, the soldier's emotion, they would turn back to loving humility, to 'humble love' where resentment and revenge have no life. Knowing what his feeling for Desdemona has been, however bloody his thoughts may be now, Othello also knows that if he thinks of his life as a happy lover dedicated to the soft, delicate servitude of his lady, they will never be swallowed in a 'capable and full revenge'.

Othello is speaking ostensibly in answer to Iago's 'Patience, I say; your mind may change'. But he is not really trying to convince Iago that he will never change; instead he is expressing both his emotions and his objective. He is feeling not jealousy but hatred; and his objective is revenge. There is no place for patience in his mind. Humility and patience are not the salves which he wants for his hurt pride; all that he will let himself consider is vengeance. He must cast love out and fill his thoughts with hatred.

An equally unchanging purpose, but a gentler one, an

expression of love not of hatred, comes from Julia in *The Two Gentlemen of Verona*. Again there is concentration on the way in which a current reaches its goal inescapably in the first half of the simile; but this way is a gentle, loving, devious one, not a swift, violent dash.

> The current that with gentle murmur glides,
> Thou know'st, being stopp'd, impatiently doth rage;
> But when his fair course is not hindered,
> He makes sweet music with th' enamell'd stones,
> Giving a gentle kiss to every sedge
> He overtaketh in his pilgrimage;
> And so by many winding nooks he strays,
> With willing sport, to the wild ocean.

Here, while Julia is describing the stream, she is really expressing the quality of her own love, and of her intention to reach her goal. Having established firmly what happens to the stream, while thinking of her love, she now concentrates explicitly, not obliquely, on her own intentions:

> Then let me go, and hinder not my course.
> I'll be as patient as a gentle stream,
> And make a pastime of each weary step,
> Till the last step have brought me to my love;
> And there I'll rest as, after much turmoil,
> A blessed soul doth in Elysium.
>
> (II, vii, 25–38)

The actress has not quite such an easy task here as has the actor of Othello. Language is not used quite so precisely; the correspondence between the first and second halves of the comparison is not so exact. For while the current of the first part 'strays/With willing sport to the wild ocean', Julia says she herself will rest when she has reach'd her love 'as, after much turmoil/A blessed soul doth in Elysium'. Leaving apart the possibility of emending 'wild' to 'wide', the actress will solve her problem by thinking of the ocean in itself as something free and vital. While the stream is not turbulent in its course, Julia for all her outward patience will have been undergoing turmoil. She is not really unperturbed herself, however little she may perturb others; this is what emerges from the discrepancy between the 'wild ocean' and resting after turmoil like a soul in bliss.

Whenever the actor's difficulties are connected with the unrealistic style of the text, he will find help in carefully mastering the surface sense of his lines as the first step to knowing the emotion they express and the objective they reveal. This is particularly true of the very unrealistic lines in which the very real meeting of Romeo and Juliet has been imagined by Shakespeare. Both actor and actress nowadays find themselves affected by the romantic tradition of a deep and overwhelming love, which sweeps the two young people away in its path; and this is the way in which only too often the modern actor and actress want to play the lines, perhaps because only such a conception of the awakening of this love can make sense of the incident for the modern mind. It seems as if safety lies only in a flaming intensity of passionate sincerity, in which reason and everyday thinking have no part. But the lines will not let the actors play them in this way successfully. The encounter is actually composed formally as a sonnet with octave and sestet; Romeo makes his first advances in the first quatrain; they are evaded by Juliet in the second; after a fresh attempt in the beginning of the sestet, Romeo eventually gains his immediate objective in the final couplet which is also the conventional resolution of the subject of a sonnet. Romeo's intellect is engaged as well as his passion; he is certainly sincerely in love with as little as he knows of Juliet, quite confident that all that he shall ever experience of peace and joy in life is dependent on winning the love of this, to him, truly angelic lady. When he first saw her his determination in touching hers to 'make blessed my rude hand' expressed more than a conventional Petrarchan conceit; he had a vision at that moment of what his life had been, and what it would be in the future without her love, and of what it could be in that same future blessed with her benevolence.

This is what Romeo is working for, his own sanity, his own bliss, when he first addresses Juliet. But circumstances do not allow him to make an open and passionate declaration; they do, however, let him take advantage of the conventional elegant badinage appropriate to conversation before the unmasking—the kind of badinage which is indulged in *Love's Labour's Lost* and *Much Ado About Nothing*. The surface sense of his first quatrain amounts, therefore, to a declaration that if she objects to his hand touching hers he is ready to pay her compensation in the shape of a kiss (on her hand, not her lips).

> If I profane with my unworthiest hand
> This holy shrine, the gentle fine is this:
> My lips, two blushing pilgrims, ready stand
> To smooth that rough touch with a tender kiss.

It must be remembered that whatever else the actor does, he must speak this sense in a way which will in his opinion lead to the attaining of his objective, and that is not just a kiss, but Juliet as the centre and salvation of his earthly life. The implications of the imagery, that he is a pilgrim and she a saint, as they are in play in the mask, allow him to be light and jesting on the surface while really expressing what he sincerely feels at the same time. When preparing to play this passage, moreover, the actor may possibly be helped by noticing clearly how the antithetical ideas and emotions are expressed in the structure of the lines. 'Profane'—'the gentle fine'; 'unworthiest hand'—'lips'; 'this holy shrine'—'two blushing pilgrims'; 'smooth'—'rough'; 'rough touch'—'tender kiss'. Finally, it may be observed that the acting (which includes the speaking) of this passage by the actor ought to be such as makes the actress playing

Juliet want to answer in the lines given to her by Shake-speare. If he and she are both playing as they should, then Shakespeare's lines, unrealistic as they are, will be the only way possible for her to express the reality of her reaction to Romeo's advances.

Juliet's mind, too, is engaged in her reply; in fact her emotions have hardly been touched as yet. She neither concedes the kiss, nor takes umbrage, allowing disdain to deal with him summarily, but enters wittily into his game. Romeo has taken advantage of social convention; he says what he really feels, protected by the convention that people do not really feel what they avow with such depth of protestation in such circumstances. And Juliet assumes that he does not really feel she is the saint of his pilgrimage. The surface sense of her quatrain amounts to an insistence that there is no need for him to offer to kiss her hand as compensation for touching it. Keeping up the relationship of pilgrim and saint, lightly and humorously, she reminds him that pilgrims are allowed to touch a saint's hands, therefore his hand has done no wrong, he need offer no compensation, it has done what is entirely fitting as an act of devotion, and in any case as 'palm to palm is holy palmers' kiss' the touch in itself would have been compensation enough, had any been required.

> Good pilgrim, you do wrong your hand too much,
> Which mannerly devotion shows in this;
> For saints have hands that pilgrims' hands do touch,
> And palm to palm is holy palmers' kiss.

In the structure of the sonnet (each speaker has had one quatrain) they have now come to the *volta*, or pause; this is the point at which the idea put forward and discussed from one point of view in the octave, is ready to be considered from another angle in the last six lines, the sestet, so that some kind of a resolution may be reached. In this case, Romeo's request that he may kiss her hand has not been successful, but he has interested her, primarily by his manner and his badinage, yet also as a likeable person worth knowing more of. On the surface he has failed in his immediate object, to kiss her hand. The sonnet structure fits that of the veiled contest between them; making use of new rhymes (as a sonneteer should), Shakespeare lets Romeo try again, with a new approach. Instead of being brought to a standstill by her refusal, he takes up her remark that 'palm to palm is holy palmers' kiss', still quite inoffensively, and—on the surface—lightly:

> Have not saints lips, and holy palmers too?

But Juliet evades this with the admission that they have, but for praying, not for kissing:

> Ay, pilgrim, lips that they must use in pray'r.

At this point Romeo's real need begins to show beneath the surface of conventional masking. He now addresses her as 'dear saint' and means it; he remembers his life without her, dreading it without her in the future, although superficially he is still lightly carrying on the conceit of a pilgrim supplicating to a saint:

> O, then, dear saint, let lips do what hands do!
> They pray; grant thou, lest faith turn to despair.

Suddenly Juliet has a flash of understanding of what she is and can be to this man; there was real despair in his voice when he expressed his fear of despair; there was real entreaty behind his mask, in his eyes, in his voice, his attitude; he needs her and makes her know it. The refusal on her lips is qualified as she feels the strength and sincerity of his emotion. This is not a game; he really needs her as a saint, and already supplicates to her in his need. And so she answers

> Saints do not move, though grant for prayers' sake.

119

The resolution of the sonnet comes now as Romeo completes its final couplet, in quiet and urgent intensity:

Then move not while my prayer's effect I take.

And this said, he kisses her on her lips.

What started as a game for her, elegant and not without dignity, has been transformed by the glimpse she has been given of his real and desperate need. The brief but intense contact of their minds has taught her that marriage can be so much more than 'an honour that I dream not of'. She had assumed that love and marriage are everyday matters of social arrangement, that there is nothing more to them; but now, suddenly, she has learned that love can be a purifying, regenerative force, redeeming a suitor from despair, from real not conventional despair, and ennobling the lady who gives. She has an understanding of the flatness and colour-lessness of a life without this love; she has glimpsed the splendour of loving and being loved, and understands the frustration of a life which does not know this love.

When Romeo's meeting with Juliet is prepared along lines such as I have suggested here, the actor does not have to speak light superficial lines with a sincerity and passion which they will not bear; and the actress does not have to learn to evoke in herself an overwhelming, but fundament-ally irrational and inexplicable love for a man who means nothing to her. When the sonnet structure is taken into account she finds herself learning to know Romeo; their minds are engaged; she learns to pity his desolation, she finds herself longing to give meaning to his life; and she lets him kiss her because she has seen in a flash that he is a pil-grim in need of what she can give him; she can rely on his faith, she will not dash it into despair; she has no doubts of his sincere love, she is certain that in the modern common-place (but none the less true here) they are 'made for each other'. As we look back at this sonnet, examining its surface sense before thinking about implications and objectives, we see that the unrealistic medium has been used subtly and powerfully to express real emotion, a real encounter between two human beings, who emerge from it different from the state in which they entered.

This meeting of Romeo and Juliet has often been declared too poetic to be really dramatic; Shakespeare is charged with not having learnt yet to distinguish between poetry and drama; he has not yet been able to extricate himself from what are more essentially poetic than dramatic interests, so the argument runs. Although we have seen that in fact the incident is dramatic as well as poetic, the objection might still be raised that a more realistic way of doing what he has done could and ought to have been tried. Nevertheless, the actor is not primarily concerned with this aspect of Shakespeare study. It is true that he ought not to close his mind to the critical appreciation of Shakespeare's art, or lack of art; but his main task is to act Shakespeare; and no matter in how many other ways this meeting might have been written, the actor has this particular one to deal with; instead of deploring the unrealistic technique, he has to use it; he must not be deterred by it; his task is to find and to evoke in himself the real emotion expressed in the unrealistic lines.

It is here that the actor must make a sharp distinction between his art and that of the literary critic. What the critic has to say about style should obviously not be ignored in itself; but it should be ignored in preparation, whenever it brings the actor to the point at which he finds it impossible or increasingly difficult to relate the unrealistic surface of style to the reality of the emotional life which he must live when playing the character. Here lies the great danger for the actor in what literary critics say about the differences of style to be detected in Shakespeare's work at different stages of his artistic development. We are commonly told, for instance, that he uses more figures in the earlier than in the later plays; but I would prefer to say that he uses them

121

differently in each phase, rather than that early plays necessarily contain more figures than late ones. In the early plays they are more obtrusive for the modern reader, and to the uninstructed modern mind they are less easily noticed in the later. But the actor needs to notice the figures, either as patterns of words and sounds, or as expressions of sense and meaning, whether the play is early or late. He should not try to ignore the figures when he has seen them in the early work, and he may often draw help from noticing them in the later.

It cannot be disputed, however, that the obtrusiveness of the figures in Shakespeare's earlier work certainly presents the actor with difficulties. The modern feeling tends to be that the figures are there for their own sake, for an extra-dramatic reason; but this feeling can lead to a dangerous attitude to the text. Only too often we shall find ourselves helping Shakepeare when he has already done much better without our help. I am not suggesting that he never makes mistakes, never is too poetic, but it is safer and, easier really, to assume that we are obtuse rather than that he is undramatic. The case which we have considered in *Romeo and Juliet* should warn us that 'poetic' and unrealistic literary technique does not invariably mean undramatic imagining with him. Often the emotion is real and most powerful where the language is most mannered. The actor must remember that it is not his task to deliver literary judgments, but it is his vocation (and I use the word wittingly) to create character; and this means that he has to present the speeches in their unrealistic quality, and at the same time to feel and express the character's feeling truthfully and completely.

Again *Romeo and Juliet* gives us our example. The time when Friar Lawrence is most violently moved, when his emotion is true and real, is when his speech is least realistic and most mannered, both in its structure and its style. 'Hold thy desperate hand,' he thunders when Romeo attempts

122

suicide. And anger and disgust pour from him, but in a speech which is built up in clearly defined sections, each of which is individually constructed in similar clearly defined sections in its turn; superficially either Shakespeare, or his character, seems more concerned with the manner of saying something than with the burning need to say it because it must be said (III, iii, 108–158).

Even so there is no missing the anger and disgust of the first sub-section.

> Art thou a man? Thy form cries out thou art:
> Thy tears are womanish; thy wild acts denote
> The unreasonable fury of a beast.

The lapse from manhood is at the centre of the Friar's disgust; a lapse which shows itself in womanly tears and the literally irrational violence of an animal. There are three clear stages of statement, showing the descent from manliness, through womanliness, into brutishness, but the Friar does not think out his points; they are not what mainly occupies his mind, but they are indispensable to the expression of the exact quality of the anger and disgust which he cannot suppress. One point hurries upon the neck of the other, impelled by the speed and violence of his sense of outrage. And sin is the only thing that can anger Friar Lawrence; he is in truth a 'holy Franciscan Friar', one whose order enjoins that to the servant of God 'nothing should be displeasing save sin'.[1] And Romeo's is a particularly brutish sin; it is a denial of manhood, both in its shedding of tears and in the desperate violence of trying to stab himself, which is a repudiation of manly fortitude.

This immediate outburst from the old man culminates in the next two lines:

> Unseemly woman in a seeming man!
> And ill-beseeming beast in seeming both!

[1] *The Writings of Saint Francis of Assisi*, tr. and ed. Father Paschal Robinson (1906), p. 13.

These owe much of their force to the compression arising from the figures which give such precision and vigour to the disgust. There is the antithesis 'woman'–'man' on which is based the play on 'unseemly', 'seeming' and 'ill-beseeming'. The disgust, almost inexpressible, becomes miraculously articulate as it denounces the descent from manliness, which makes Romeo seem a woman in an unseemly way and at the same time to seem, and not to be, a man in his male form; and as his seeming to be both man and woman (man in his form, woman in his tears) has led to his attempted act of violence, to seem both man and woman in this way is to be an ill-beseeming beast. This is the sense compressed into so few words; but the compression makes these words a flaming expression of the emotion carried in the sense.

In the next section of the speech the Friar tries to reason with Romeo. There is the same shocked disapproval, but the appalling sin does not draw the same force of anger now:

> Thou hast amaz'd me. By my holy order,
> I thought thy disposition better temper'd.

And again there is an outburst in a figured passage, which has real emotion if expressed in an unrealistic style. The repetition of 'slain', 'slay', 'slay' and the contrast between 'slay' and 'life', 'lives' express a disgust with the very idea of killing:

> Hast thou slain Tybalt? Wilt thou slay thyself?
> And slay thy lady that in thy life lives,
> By doing damned hate upon thyself?

Have you not had enough slaughter, he asks; cannot you stop with Tybalt, must you go on and kill yourself, and thus kill one more, your lady, by killing yourself? There seems to me to be a burning sarcasm in this speech; but a sarcasm which expresses sincere feeling. For the Friar the phrase 'damned hate' may be conventional, but it is also literally true; it is a damned hate, the opposite of the blessed love in which he believes, and in the spirit of which he married Romeo and Juliet that they might end damned hatred in Verona.

The compressed style of the next section also allows much to be said with passion and sincerity:

Why railest thou on thy birth, the heaven and earth?
Since birth, and heaven, and earth, all three do meet
In thee at once; which thou at once wouldst lose.

The pattern 'all three'—'at once'—'at once' concentrates attention on the fact that Romeo would nullify in one blow, at one moment, what is the result of so much coming together in one point. The repetition of 'birth', 'heaven', 'earth' is capable of expansion into the tremendous realization that Romeo is a man, born to inherit the earth, born to proceed to heaven, with much more that these statements imply inevitably. And it is this birthright of such mighty potentialities that Romeo would repudiate and nullify in one single moment of rashness.

To strain against the figurative patterns is to run into difficulties in the next section, which in its careful construction might well suggest that the Friar is enjoying argument and verbiage. While I doubt if Shakespeare wants us to see Lawrence as a prosy old man enjoying his skill in debate, I think that what is happening here is that the speech is constructed in a sermon-like manner because the Friar is trying in the best way known to him to shame Romeo into recognizing himself, to reclaim him and make him act like a man so that he shall not let his passion destroy him utterly. Here the speaker is fundamentally disappointed that one endowed with such advantages in being a man, and even more in being so splendid a man in youth and beauty, should cast them away; this is worse than to fall into sin for the want of such advantages.

> Fie, fie! Thou shamest thy shape, thy love, thy wit;
> Which, like a usurer, abound'st in all,
> And usest none in that true use indeed
> Which should bedeck thy shape, thy love, thy wit.

The first four lines introduce a bitter harangue; with shape, love and reason, all of which are human and man-like, Romeo reduces them to something which denies his humanity, his manliness: instead of using this wealth to enhance humanity he misuses it in desecration. And when the Friar comes to deplore how each of the qualities is distorted into abuse, the negation of such potential virtue, to the fostering of which his whole life is dedicated, leads to a bitter grief in which admiration and outrage are effectively and powerfully expressed by the antithetical figures:

> Thy noble shape is but a form of wax,
> Digressing from the valour of a man;
> Thy dear love sworn but hollow perjury,
> Killing that love which thou hast vow'd to cherish;
> Thy wit, that ornament to shape and love,
> Misshapen in the conduct of them both,
> Like powder in a skilless soldier's flask,
> Is set afire by thine own ignorance,
> And thou dismemb'red with thine own defence.

By 'wit' the Friar means the judging part of the human soul; 'wit' here is a synonym for 'judgement' or 'understanding'. His play on words does not denote a constitutional delight in rhetorical figures; this is the way in which the dramatist makes his character express a sincere disapproval as he deplores the fact that so much can be reduced to so little.

His denunciation and disapproval having had their day, the Friar now tries to console Romeo by enumerating the points in which he ought to rejoice:

126

What, rouse thee, man! Thy Juliet is alive,
For whose dear sake thou wast but lately dead;
There art thou happy. Tybalt would kill thee,
But thou slewest Tybalt; there art thou happy too.
The law, that threat'ned death, becomes thy friend,
And turns it to exile; there art thou happy.

And now in the simile of 'a misbehav'd and sullen wench'
the Friar says just what he has been feeling about Romeo's
utter abandonment to grief.

Happiness courts thee in her best array;
But, like a misbehav'd and sullen wench,
Thou pout'st upon thy fortune and thy love.

Although the Friar's disapproval of Romeo becomes less
fiery as the speech continues, the actor must no doubt have
a feeling of increasing exasperation with the futility of trying to rouse the young man out of his self-centred grief, now
almost become apathy. Only when the Friar says what
Romeo wants to hear is there any real contact; only then is
he sympathizing with the miserable lover, sharing his joy
that not all has been lost.

Two lines in this speech express the core of the Friar's
attitude to life; bitterly he declares:

Which like a usurer abound'st in all,
And usest none in that true use indeed.

He sees Romeo's behaviour as one more example of the
effect of the Fall on Creation which he deplored in his
opening speech (II, iii, 1–30). After rejoicing that there is
nothing alive on the earth that is too vile to bestow some
good upon it, he grieves that the reverse is also true:

O, mickle is the powerful grace that lies
In plants, herbs, stones, and their true qualities;
For nought so vile that on the earth doth live

127

But to the earth some special good doth give;
Nor aught so good but, strain'd from that fair use,
Revolts from true birth, stumbling on abuse.

Not only these sentiments, but the whole of this speech is entirely consistent with the teaching of the Franciscan Order. Friar Lawrence is all too easily dismissed here as speaking in dull, prosy verse, with too much periphrasis, repetition and sententious commonplace. But the actor ought to ignore such prejudice and first look at the sense of the words before trying to imagine what he is to feel and express. The first four lines describe dawn coming up brightly in the face of night's darkness. Once the eastern sky has been streaked with light, the darkness withdraws fitfully from the steady and swift approach of day:

The gray-ey'd morn smiles on the frowning night,
Check'ring the eastern clouds with streaks of light;
And fleckel'd darkness like a drunkard reels
From forth day's path and Titan's fiery wheels.

The image of morn smiling and night frowning is commonplace enough, but that does not stop it from expressing, not only what the actor must imagine himself seeing, but what he is actually to feel as he speaks the words. Night for him is 'frowning'; he does not love it; but he rejoices in day; it smiles for him personally, so that the conventional epithet expresses what he really feels. The Franciscan poem known as *The Canticle of the Sun* has similar sentiments to those of these four lines, indeed, is similar in tone to the speech as a whole, and is also known as *Praises of the Creatures*. Night is not actually mentioned with dislike explicitly, but the moon and stars are celebrated, together with fire, for lighting up the dark; and praise in particular is given to 'my brother sun' for lighting the day, with a brightness and radiance given by, and significant of, God.[1] And so Friar

[1]Ed. Robinson, *op. cit.*, pp. 152 f.

Lawrence rejoices at the sight of the sun driving on radiantly and dispelling darkness.

This Franciscan follows his teacher, the founder of his Order, when he celebrates the world and the individual creatures that live and die on the earth, each having some virtue to impart. But, as the *Canticle* cries 'Woe to them who die in mortal sin',[1] so Friar Lawrence after exulting in the fact of Grace, denounces sin which is punished by 'the canker death'. Early in the speech he remarks on his task to 'up-fill' his basket not only with 'baleful weeds' but also with 'precious-juiced flowers'; and for him the two are interchangeable; for he knows that in life nothing is too vile to be of some good use, and nothing is too good to be distorted into doing harm. Like fallen humanity, the weak flower is capable of good and evil; everywhere the struggle goes on between 'grace and rude will', in nature as well as in man.

The speech does express thoughts and feelings which are vital to the Friar; there is a genuine awareness of man as potentially a blessed or a damned spirit; this is an awareness which is always with him, and from it come sincerely the exultant and despondent feelings expressed in the speech. An actor who has really looked at the surface sense can then begin to know its implications and feel the emotions which they give rise to. Without making the assertion explicitly the Friar is implying powerfully that the world being what it is, he is dedicated to the service of God; the speech is in essence an act of worship. When this has been grasped and the words are spoken to do for the actor what they do for the Friar, the lines lose their apparent stiffness and dullness. Epigrammatic as the style is in its compression, the fact that much is said in comparatively few words in the individual couplets means that conviction and emotion are concentrated.

What the Friar has to say is very important for the understanding of Shakespeare's theme: honour is in itself a virtue;

[1] *Ibid.*, p. 153.

but when it is abused, as in the feud between the Montagues and the Capulets, it becomes a vice. If allowed to, this distorted sense of honour would destroy public order in Verona completely and even lead to the disintegration of the state. Here again is conflict between grace and rude will. But Providence works through Fortune and the human beings, particularly through the lovers, to a reconciliation of the two families, which is brought about by the unhappy marriage of their children. Because the speech is of such importance, and because it is dull at first sight, an actor may easily be tempted into thinking that Shakespeare was more concerned with his use of Friar Lawrence than with drawing completely a likeable and live character. But I think it has been shown that there is more to the Friar than is apparent at first sight, and that he is not depicted, here at least, as a blundering, sententious bore. Nevertheless the fact that he is important to the plot throughout the action coupled with another fact, that his lines are written in a difficult style according to modern notions, may easily intensify a suspicion that the character has been superficially drawn, and that Shakespeare was concerned mostly with having a character who can help to hurry along his action for him.

Romeo and Juliet must be married in secret, so a father-confessor supplies a need. Somebody must plan for Romeo to take refuge in Mantua, to keep in contact with him, and prepare the way for his pardon; somebody is needed to think out the desperate plan with Juliet, to give her the drug, to superintend her interment, to send a message to Romeo, to give an account of the whole affair so that the two families shall know what has been happening and end their feud. And the Friar meets each of Shakespeare's needs.

At the same time as we recognize the Friar's function in the mechanism of the plot, we remark on what seem like lapses in the drawing of him. In particular he seems to have no hesitations, no qualms, when actually making the decision to marry the lovers. There is no suggestion that he is

130

running any risk, that any unfortunate consequences might occur, either for himself or for anybody else. After refusing to take Romeo seriously, he suddenly decides:

> But come, young waverer, come, go with me,
> In one respect I'll thy assistant be;
> For this alliance may so happy prove
> To turn your households' rancour to pure love.
>
> (II, iii, 89–92)

This is not the blind decision of an irresponsible optimist completely oblivious to the difficulties in what he is doing; Friar Lawrence is not in any way irresponsible, although his behaviour might seem to be. His responsibility to his Creator is to promote peace, to reconcile enemies. One of the most dearly held principles of the Franciscan rule is summed up in the lines from Matthew 5: 3, which is quoted in the fifteenth Admonition of St. Francis on the religious life: 'Blessed are the peacemakers: for they shall be called the children of God.'[1] The saint himself preached with practical effect against civil war within city states as well as against inter-city strife; and his followers were firm opponents of the same evils, never losing a chance of promoting peace and reconciliation. And so, a true Franciscan, Friar Lawrence cares primarily for what is most important, so long as it can be achieved without sin—that is the turning of the households' 'rancour to pure love'.

Unworldly rather than incompetent and blundering is the word to be used of the Friar. He does not think things out in detail, anticipating difficulties and dangers and preparing alternative plans if his schemes should go astray. With sublime, not stupid, confidence he rejoices in looking forward to the time when he will reconcile Romeo's friends,

> Beg pardon of the Prince, and call thee back
> With twenty hundred thousand times more joy
> Than thou went'st forth in lamentation.

[1] *Op. cit.*, p. 14.

131

This expresses his genuine happiness in the thought of peace and of happiness for others. He is happy now, partly in that he can see an immediate, if temporary, reunion for Romeo and Juliet, partly in his certainty that they will eventually be reunited more permanently, but most of all in his vision of two reconciled, instead of warring, families. And knowing his man, he warns Romeo not to risk capture by staying a little longer than is safe with Juliet.

Friar Lawrence has his second real shock when he hears from Paris of Old Capulet's intentions (IV, 1, 1–17). Not having expected this he has no plan; he has been caught completely unprepared. We might expect him to consider the possibility of revealing the secret marriage; but Shakespeare has followed tradition in assuming that this is unthinkable and needs the Friar to propose the desperate expedient to Juliet. If the actor remembers the unworldliness of the character and the overwhelming desire to reconcile the families and to avoid sin, it will be easier not to feel that here is more shallow blundering by a sententious dodderer. This time the resolution to commit suicide by one of the lovers does not reduce the Friar to the same outraged anger at the possibility of such a sin. Juliet's resolution is so much more deliberate than her husband's; she remembers that 'God joined my heart and Romeo's, thou our hands', and her resolution is to preserve her marriage from desecration. She is prepared to accept 'some present counsel'; and her determination not to betray her vows and her readiness to turn to him for help are so reasonable that instead of invoking in him horror of suicide, they awaken the glimmering of

> a kind of hope,
> Which craves as desperate an execution
> As that is desperate which we would prevent.

His plan is breath-takingly audacious and requires an iron nerve, both in Juliet and the Friar. Her nerve is not of iron;

but he is right in relying on her devotion and her determination to 'live an unstain'd wife to my sweet love'. Again the Friar busies himself about the practical details of this plan to retrieve the position; and again he does not dwell on the possibilities of failure or try to anticipate anything going awry. And he remembers to send a friar with speed to warn Romeo. The nearest Friar Lawrence comes to deceitful scheming and intrigue is when he plays his part in tricking the Capulets; again his whole concern is with reuniting the separated husband and wife; and his admonition to the parents in what they think is their bereavement is not something which he enjoys with his tongue in his cheek, although it is something which the actor must feel happy to know is not really needed. The Friar can act when he has to, but he does not plan comprehensively, and his activity is piecemeal. Again he is caught unawares when he hears that the message did not reach Romeo; there is the same shock, the sense of being involved in something which is too big for him; but again he quickly stoops to pick up the pieces, resolving at once to go to Juliet and save her, planning already to hide her and let Romeo know later. He does not dawdle, sends immediately for the crowbar and is off. Yet it is for him the same kind of effort as there was for Juliet in taking the drug. When he finds Balthasar and the page refuses to accompany him, he is seized with fear, yet makes himself go on, now severely shaken. When Juliet awakens and he hears approaching noises, the Friar is completely unnerved; now he recognizes that he was dabbling in something which he did not understand:

A greater power than we can contradict
Hath thwarted our intents.

This is not empty commonplace but sincere conviction.

By the time that the Friar has been found and brought before the Prince he has become a shattered, horrified old man, suffering physically from his exertions, suffering mentally from the failure of his good intentions, feeling personally inadequate (although he is never proud and self-satisfied) and convinced that Heaven's plans have thwarted his. Trembling, sighing, and weeping, almost completely exhausted, feeling himself at death's door, whether he is, in fact, or not, he makes a supreme effort to show exactly what has been going on. His last speech, made in the presence of the Prince and the whole city, must not be regarded as an incompletely dramatic expedient to round off the story. The Friar is re-experiencing what has happened to him; as he relates the story of Romeo and Juliet, he feels keenly his inability to save them, remembering each stage of the inevitable advance of events to this moment, feeling over again the sickening sense of failure as each plan went wrong, the futile hope that each successive expedient, each with less chance of success, might avert what he now knows was inevitable. Shakespeare is using the actor for two purposes now; first to re-awaken in the audience more acutely the memories of what they felt as the play developed, and to make them feel the way in which the tragedy could not be avoided, given these people in these circumstances; the second purpose is to move the citizens of Verona while informing them of what has happened, so that the two families can be reconciled in their grief. But the actor will not do Shakespeare's work, will not achieve these two aims, unless he feels the emotions proper to the broken, exhausted old man, unless he experiences the events which relates as something which happened to him. By identifying himself with Friar Lawrence, moreover, he will make this speech intensely moving.

We have already noted the difficulty which the style of the dialogue given to the Friar creates for the modern actor when we consider the reaction to Romeo's attempt at suicide. The earlier part of this scene is written in much the same style, which tends to obstruct the modern actor trying to decide on the emotion he should feel and the objective for which he should strive. As he tries to reason with Romeo here, too, the Friar seems devoid of feeling, incapable of sympathizing with Romeo, concerned more with decorating his sententiously empty substitutes for consolation than with really helping his pupil in his sorrows. His first lines as the scene opens might easily be interpreted as unctuous revelling in the calamity which has descended on Romeo.

> Romeo, come forth; come forth, thou fearful man;
> Affliction is enamour'd of thy parts,
> And thou art wedded to calamity.

The literal sense of the last two lines is 'Affliction has fallen in love with your physical and mental qualities and you have married calamity.' But this is not a heartless joke; for the implications of the sense are that Juliet almost personifies affliction in her distress, and that at the same time as he has been claimed by calamity and affliction for the rest of his life, Romeo's marriage is to someone in the same situation. The Friar is ruminating bitterly, moved by their troubles. At this moment he will not hide from himself the full unhappiness of the circumstances; nor will he hide it from Romeo; for his intention is to save his pupil from despair, not by glossing over his troubles, but by making him recognize them and exercise fortitude in enduring them. But he insists that things could be worse. Romeo has been given a gentler judgement, "Not body's death, but body's banishment.' This does not have the effect the Friar hopes for, and so he reminds Romeo that he is banished only from Verona, urges him to be patient for the world is not only large, but it is all open to him ('wide'); 'wide' is not tautologous; it does not have the sense of broad, but of open and unbarred.

> Here from Verona art thou banished.
> Be patient, for the world is broad and wide.

Romeo's reply evokes anger in the Friar, now; true to his

order he reserves anger for nothing but sin. He does not temporize with Romeo when tact might accomplish more, but uncompromisingly denounces the sin, insisting:

> This is dear mercy, and thou seest it not.

Wresting with Romeo now the Friar is unable to make real contact: he is confronted with an agony that will not respond to his certainties. What he says is true; but in Romeo's present anguish it is useless:

> I'll give thee armour to keep off that word;
> Adversity's sweet milk, philosophy,
> To comfort thee, though thou art banished.

His objective is still to console Romeo, to save him from the sin of despair; both his affection for the individual and his duty as a servant of God fight with his sense of exasperation to keep his temper, which has almost flared up in his words, a few moments earlier:

> Thou fond mad man, hear me a little speak.

But when Romeo refuses to hear him or his philosophy (naturally enough in the circumstances) the Friar's temper gives way:

> O, then I see that madmen have no ears.

But he recovers it again and tries in the only way he knows:

> Let me dispute with thee of thy estate.

If he could get Romeo to argue with him he might do some good, and he knows it; but this is not the way. But he feels no smug superiority; he is trying in the best way he knows, thinking only of Romeo and not of his own knowledge or skill in debate, to console, to save from the sin of despair. His fundamental kindness and humanity show themselves when, as his anger at Romeo's attempted suicide simmers down, he suddenly takes one of his decisions which are so disconcerting when we realize their audacity which does not seem to give him any qualms at all, almost as if he is not aware of what it is he is advising; he is always looking (without qualifications or second thoughts) at the immediate end which is worth striving for.

To the mixture of elements which make up the Friar an actor must add his gentle tolerance of human frailty when mortal sin is not involved. In the encounter with Romeo after Romeo has exchanged vows with Juliet, the Friar shows this gentle and affectionate side of his nature. And nothing is more expressive of his warm personal relationship with Romeo than the sudden switch from general moralizing to:

> Or if not so, then here I hit it right—
> Our Romeo hath not been in bed tonight.

And there is the same sense of fun, by no means conflicting with his underlying seriousness in his parodying of Romeo's recent lamentations for lack of Rosaline's favours.

An actor who reads the text without prejudice and bases his decisions as to objective and emotions on considering the literal sense of the words before proceeding to implications, will find many elements to be incorporated into a portrayal of Friar Lawrence which might otherwise escape him. He will also find the Friar's dialogue expressive of real emotion when it is by no means realistic. This again is true for the actress of Juliet, one of whose most deeply emotional outbursts is expressed by means of word-play and other figures. Yet what she says to the Nurse is almost literally true:

> Say thou but 'I',
> And that bare vowel 'I' shall poison more
> Than the death-darting eye of cockatrice.

The structure of this passage balances damage done by the affirmative given in one bare vowel against that done by the eye of the cockatrice; and not only is 'I' balanced against 'eye', but the qualifying 'bare vowel' has an equivalent in 'of cockatrice'. The whole passage is expressive of extreme bitterness as well as grief; Juliet feels the irony of a simple 'I' (meaning 'yes') doing such damage; it almost literally poisons her, it certainly will be no less effective than poison; the hyperbole may not be literally true, but it is a true expression of her very real feelings. There is the same pitiful truth, indeed now she speaks what is literally true as well, in her

> I am not I, if there be such an 'I'.

By creating the bare vowel affirmative the Nurse will be annihilating Juliet; the compression of the antithesis and the repeated pun on 'I' are not substitutes for feeling: the structure of this line allows the actress to concentrate her emotion precisely, and express its overwhelming intensity in what is logically clear and inescapable: structurally the unit 'I am not' is balanced against 'there be', and 'I' against 'such an I'. And formal as the couplet is, the emotion is not; the emotion floods out to a bitter culmination as she implores to be put out of her uncertainty, even if it is an answer which she dreads:

> If he be slain, say 'I'; or if not, 'No';
> Brief sounds determine of my weal or woe.

This scene shows the second of Juliet's thorough testings; consequences and situations which she has imagined as possible now present themselves in reality. When she first realized what her relationship with Romeo might be she soon faced in her mind the consequences of falling in love with and then marrying a Montague. Now she finds, indeed, that her husband is more to her than anything else in the world, that her family and her friends are nothing weighed against him; he is the centre of her life, all that matters in living:

> My husband lives that Tybalt would have slain,
> And Tybalt's dead that would have slain my husband.

138

There really is comfort for her in these words; the patterning of 'my husband' at the beginning and end of these two lines, the repetitions of 'Tybalt' and 'would have slain', and the antithesis 'lives'—'dead' express a real comfort born out of the facing of the awful fact of Tybalt's death and of the still more awful possibility that the death could have been Romeo's had it not been Tybalt's. The quality of her love for Romeo which wipes out all other considerations as paltry, gives rise to the stricken bitterness which tears itself out of her as she contrasts 'one' with 'ten thousand', and 'word' with 'Tybalts':

> That 'banished', that one word 'banished',
> Hath slain ten thousand Tybalts.

And in the lines which follow, Shakespeare's art, unrealistic as it is, does not destroy the reality of Juliet's emotion. Normally those who are 'sour' do not want company, but this woe perversely seems to have wanted more than Tybalt's death and apparently 'delights in fellowship'. Why, then, she asks were not her relatives, Romeo and herself all taken, for that would be less than to pronounce Romeo banished; again the couplet allows the emotion to rise to a culminating point.

> There is no end, no limit, measure, bound,
> In that word's death; no words can that woe sound.

And the last word 'sound' not only means to 'give voice to' but to 'measure the depth of'. But Juliet's use of the pun does not indicate delight in punning; Shakespeare has used it to express her overwhelming grief, her certainty that without her husband's living presence the rest of the world and she herself are as dead.

All this was implied even though Juliet had not given name to these implications when in her reverie, thinking herself alone, she asserted that the feud would never come

between her and Romeo, even if it meant her leaving her
family and friends and giving all of herself to him:

> And for thy name, which is no part of thee,
> Take all myself.
>
> (II, ii, 48–49).

And, a few moments later, asking if his purpose was marriage, she declared:

> And all my fortunes at thy foot I'll lay,
> And follow thee, my lord, throughout the world.
>
> (147–8)

Now, when she has just been told some scenes later that
her cousin is dead and at her husband's hand, her earlier
repudiation of all ties but marriage is tested to the limit. At
first the killing of the man designated later 'my dearest
cousin' provokes a bitterness which swamps her love for his
killer, who is also later called 'my dearer lord', dearer, that
is, than that dearest of all cousins. The recollection of his
attraction for her does not in any way sweeten the bitterness of her denunciation of him in paradoxical figures: in
each case love and hatred are contrasted; but the dominant
emotion is regret that love should have been given to this
of all men, regret that he should have seemed worthy of it;
there is no denial of Romeo's charm and power to move her
love, but there is deep regret that such a thing could have
happened: and it is all summed up in the last words of the
speech:

> O, that deceit should dwell
> In such a gorgeous palace!

But the sound of her sentiments on another's lips horrifies
Juliet. From the outburst 'Blister'd be thy tongue' onward
there is no doubt of Juliet's resolution to keep her husband
as the centre of her life; her complete loyalty is none the
less sincere for the fact that she expresses it in a play upon
words:

> He was not born to shame:
> Upon his brow shame is asham'd to sit;
> For 'tis a throne where honour may be crown'd
> Sole monarch of the universal earth.

And the incredulous disapproval of the Nurse,

> Will you speak well of him that kill'd your cousin?

provokes the flash of stychomythia, with every word a repudiation of the disloyalty just recommended:

> Shall I speak ill of him that is my husband?

Shakespeare has brought Juliet to this point in clearly marked stages of development. First she is the young girl of marriageable age in her society who has thought no more of the bond than that it is 'an honour'. Without the slightest inkling of what is involved in 'looking to love', she calmly promises her mother that she will look at Paris ('look to' also means 'prepare') in order to like him (or, she will be prepared to like him) if looking can bring about liking; but she will not let the dart of her eye penetrate any further than it is given strength to fly by her mother's consent:

> I'll look to like, if looking liking move;
> But no more deep will I endart mine eye
> Than your consent gives strength to make it fly.
>
> (I, iii, 98–100)

The actress may find some help with these lines from remembering that when Shakespeare wrote them for Juliet it was believed that love at first sight was the result of one person's eye-beams literally entering the other through his or her eyes.

But the encounter with Romeo gives Juliet a very different relationship with a man who will never receive her parents' consent. First, she realizes the depth of her love when she tells the Nurse to ask Romeo's name, having dissembled her interest with inquiries about the other young men; she knows that this is the man for her; and so much does he mean to her that the conception of marriage as 'an honour' has been swept away by the bitter certainty:

> If he be married,
> My grave is like to be my wedding bed.
>
> (I, v, 131–2)

As Juliet learns the name of the man who has awakened this passion in her, the next stage of her development begins; from thinking of marriage as an honour in which her parents' consent plays a part, she has come to see it as something to satisfy an overwhelming need with which they are not concerned. And now her clear realization of what has happened is expressed in bitter regret that Fortune has played this trick on her:

> My only love sprung from my only hate!
> Too early seen unknown, and known too late!

The compression of the lines emphasizes what is literally true; this is the only love she has known; Romeo, the only object of her love, is the offspring of the only object of her hate; she saw him, indeed, too early, before she knew who he was; and the damage that has been done is such that it is now too late when she knows his identity; now she loves him.

> Prodigious birth of love it is to me,
> That I must love a loathed enemy.

Again she is right; what she realizes so clearly is true; the love born in her is miraculous; it is a prodigy in that she is loving one whom she has always hated (and apparently still hates) as an enemy. The compression of these two lines does not detract from their clarity; Juliet knows exactly what is happening to her; she regrets her love at this point because of the confusion which it must bring, but certain as she is that Romeo is a loathed enemy, she is also certain that she loves him. Falling in love so suddenly, despite an earlier certainty that she would do no such thing without discussing the matter with her parents, is the first stage in her emancipation from the attitudes of childhood; the next stage has now come with her avowal of love for Romeo although he is her hereditary enemy; she does not even consider attempting to smother her love for him; instead she regrets the fact that she cannot have him for her husband. She has decided that she never wants to marry anyone but the man whose despair was vanquished by her graciousness; and the fact that he is Romeo does not make her change her mind.

This is what she thinks and feels as she 'leans her cheek upon her hand', and sighs, 'Ay me!' Preparing to play this scene, the actress can muse unhappily over the unfortunate position Juliet is in, thinking how desperately unfair it is that the man must turn out to be a Montague, when it might easily, so easily, have been somebody acceptable to her family, somebody from whom she was not separated by so much shed blood. And then she will find that the words Shakespeare has given her are words which she needs at this moment, which express her emotion and her objective as she speaks them. 'Why are you, of all people, Romeo? Repudiate your stock, your side of the feud; or if you will not, I do not care so long as you will "be but sworn my love"; I will repudiate my share of our traditional enmity and act as if I were not a Capulet.'

> O Romeo, Romeo! wherefore art thou Romeo?
> Deny thy father and refuse thy name;
> Or, if thou wilt not, be but sworn my love,
> And I'll no longer be a Capulet.

She has gone one stage farther away from the girl who has unquestioningly accepted her beliefs and standards, her friends and enemies, from her family. And a minute later, her mind still full of love for Romeo, she insists to herself

143

that the mere fact that he is a Montague does not make him
her enemy, when in himself he is the man she loves. Then
she longs for him to repudiate his name, vowing that if he
would do that, give up something which is not even really a
part of the essential him, she will bestow on him all of herself. When he speaks she recognizes the voice and is both
terrified on his behalf and delighted on her own that he
should be there; in each case she is expressing her love for
him. And she makes it clear that there is no point in a pretence at coyness, and yet that her directness does not come
from a lack of modesty. There is in this speech a mixture of
modestness and open sincerity; an insistence that she will
prove more true 'Than those that have more cunning to be
strange'. And then overcome with the thought of what he
has overheard she insists again that without denying her
avowal of 'true love's passion' she is not shameless, asking
him not to impute

> this yielding to light love,
> Which the dark night hath so discovered.

The meaning of this last line and a half is well worth
studying; Juliet uses 'light' in its sense of 'not heavy'; but
uses 'dark' in antithesis to 'light' in the sense of the opposite
of dark; and while dark night usually covers things, in this
case, as she ruefully admits, it has found out and exposed
what she would prefer to have kept hidden.

Love for Juliet is no conventional matter of social obliga-
tion; it is not a matter to be treated in the light manner of
courtly convention either; she does not want Romeo to
swear by the moon or by anything but himself. She sees her
relationship with him as one in which there is no room for
subterfuge, for anything but complete giving of self in full
confidence. When Romeo asks for:

> Th' exchange of thy love's faithful vow for mine,

she replies,

> I gave thee mine before thou didst request it;
> And yet I would it were to give again.

For her joy comes from giving; all she wants is to be frank, to be generous; this being so, her pun on 'bounty' and 'boundless' helps her to express the depth of her longing to give to Romeo:

> My bounty is as boundless as the sea,
> My love as deep: the more I give to thee,
> The more I have, for both are infinite.

It is the paradox of the last line and a half that affords her greatest satisfaction.

For all her refusal to dissemble, Juliet is right in asserting that hers is not a 'light' love. It is not profane; she wants Romeo in marriage or not at all. Once she knows he has overheard, she admits her love for him; this paves the way for the next development, the readiness to marry him, to turn from all that she has known, to leave father, mother, friends, not merely for a husband, but for a husband who is their hated enemy. Her reminder that she will break off all relations with him if his purpose is not marriage is not because Juliet is thinking selfishly of catching her man; it is because she cannot contemplate a sinful relationship with him; for her, marriage now is so much more than 'an honour'; but love without marriage, a giving of herself—for nothing else is imaginable—would be foul dishonour and a sin. And so she is now ready to exchange her family for the enemy with whom she has fallen so sincerely and so maturely in love.

In this mood of confident joy, happy because she is to be united to the centre of her life, Juliet awaits her nurse, receives Romeo's message, and meets him at the Friar's cell as arranged. She is in fundamentally the same mood when she apostrophizes the 'fiery footed steeds'; but it is heightened with impatience and expectation of her happiness in her husband's arms. She is looking forward to night as the time when he can come safely, when she shall be able to have him with her in reality as he is with her now in her fantasy. No wonder that she prefers the safety and secrecy of night made splendid by him to the barren splendour of the 'garish sun'. And the love with which she awaits the joys of being married to Romeo, as we have seen, after a certain faltering, stands the test of the sorrows and confusion of loyalties which spring from that same married state.

In the scene when Romeo takes his leave of her, Juliet's very real emotion is once more expressed in word-play. When she admits to herself that it really is day, she is terrified for Romeo's safety; and so she finds herself urgently telling him to leave her, when the one thing in the world which she does not want is to be parted from him. The bitterness of this irony, the longing for him not to go and the terror for his safety if he stays, is really expressed in the figurative structure of her dialogue:

> It is the lark that sings so out of tune,
> Straining harsh discords and unpleasing sharps.

The details of this should not be allowed to transfer the actress's attention to what the words describe from what they express; they express her longing never to be separated from her husband, not a musical dislike of the lark's singing; this latter is what they describe. And her loathing of the day itself is expressed as a loathing of the bird whose voice means to her all the anguish which is brought by this particular day.

> Some say the lark makes sweet division;
> This doth not so, for she divideth us.
> Some say the lark and loathed toad change eyes;
> O, now I would that they chang'd voices too!
> Since arm from arm that voice does us affray,
> Hunting thee hence with hunts-up to the day.

And it is her love for him that speaks in the urgent fear that bids him go before it is too light to go with safety.

Now when Juliet is irrevocably Romeo's wife, she finds herself expected to go on behaving as the Capulets' child. She has resisted the pressure of hereditary hatred and of her love for her cousin to separate her from her husband; now she finds herself subjected to other pressures to which she is even more conditioned to submit. She has to defy her parents in fact, not in her mind; although she has talked of doing this, she has not actually imagined what it would be like, or really thought of it happening. Her conflict with her family is the logical result of her deliberate giving of herself in love; it distresses her, drives her almost to distraction, but it does not make her weaken in her love and loyalty to her husband. Disowned by her father unless she marries Paris, she still turns to the person on whom she has relied as a matter of course for kindness, her mother; and when her plea, 'cast me not away!' is rejected with, 'Do as thou wilt, for I have done with thee,' there is but one link left with her old life as a daughter of the Capulets. Although Juliet has never wavered in her loyalty to Romeo since hearing him cursed by her nurse, and although she has put him before her family, she has not had to face the actual hostility of her father and mother until now; she has put them aside, but has not anticipated in her mind the bitterness of being put aside by them; for her there has always been the central fact that she was not so much denying them as giving herself to Romeo; denial of them has been something linked to giving to Romeo, but she has had no need to deny them which springs from positive dislike. In fact her pre-occupation with Romeo has not permitted her even to think of separation from her family except in terms of union with him. As a result her treatment by her father and mother now appals her; she is not prepared for such violence of spirit, she has never met it and is not hardened to it; yet devastating as it is, it does not so much as suggest to her the slightest hint of weakening and repudiating Romeo, which would be so easy as he is in Mantua and their marriage is secret. Although she is 'so soft a subject', her love and loyalty to him are unassailable, even in her sudden realization of what it means to be his wife in these circumstances. But she has not yet had to cut herself completely adrift from everything which has nourished and supported her in her life before she fell in love with this 'loathed enemy'. There is still the Nurse, who has just spoken up for her against her father, and who has indulged her and helped her to marry Romeo. Again the truth of her emotion is expressed in unrealistic language involving figures of words; but Juliet needs the words to say what she must; she is at her wit's end; it is all so much harder than she expected; but so long as her husband lives she will not marry another; she asks for comfort, but the only comfort she can find is the counsel which will enable her to preserve herself for Romeo by evading her father's plan; 'how shall this be prevented?' is what occupies her mind; her objective is still to give herself to Romeo, or having made the gift once to share it with nobody else.

> My husband is on earth, my faith in heaven;
> How shall that faith return again to earth,
> Unless that husband send it me from heaven
> By leaving earth?

She is not asking how else can this happen, but expressing her conviction that there is no other way. Utter love for him which admits of no compromise is what dominates her. And now comes the final shock, which shows her how completely she is isolated, with no friend to trust where she has always turned trustingly as a matter of course; father and mother and now nurse are all divided from her; she must rely on her own powers and not weaken in her love and resolution. After the sudden decision early in the play never to marry if the man was not Romeo, Juliet has been entirely consistent as soon as circumstances have curtailed her opportunities for inconsistency. Ignoring the feud, trying to carry love for Tybalt as well as Romeo in her heart, she abandons Tybalt for her husband; having vowed that he comes before father, mother, all, she tries inconsistently to remain the daughter of the Capulets while the wife of a Montague; but again circumstances prevent her; and she allows herself to be rejected as a daughter because it is more important to her not to be faithless as a wife. Now, listening to her nurse's plan, she admits to herself that none of this household has anything for her; she is free of them at last; and on hearing that the Nurse really counsels the plan which she herself has already rejected (her rejection of it may well have put it in the Nurse's mind), a certain ruthlessness comes into her personality. Nothing and nobody is going to come between her and her husband; there remains one more possible source of help; if the Friar also fails her 'myself have power to die'. It is a remedy forced on her by the circumstances; and one which she contemplates calmly, not hysterically. She will not betray her love. If she cannot be Romeo's faithful wife she does not want to live.

This resolution supports her from now on; it is easy to deceive Paris and her nurse and parents in such a cause; in her need they mean nothing to her; first she cut herself off from them fundamentally by her love and her marriage; then their behaviour taught her what that amounted to in fact. They are nothing to her, Romeo is all; she must keep herself 'an unstain'd wife', if possible alive, but if not, dead. Sure of nothing else, feeling herself desperately weak and incapable of finding a happy way out of her troubles, she is preoccupied with her one certainty—Romeo is the centre of her life; for him she will undergo any hardship, any horror; and if the outcome is still not brought to an 'issue of true honour', she will choose death.

Thus resolved it is easy to play the malleable, repentant

daughter, to deceive her family in this holy cause. But independent as she has become, Juliet is still young and unused to independence; she was ready to exchange family for husband; now she has given up family, but she is separated from her husband; the strain of utter isolation— for now even the Friar cannot be with her—adds to the trial which she undergoes when Lady Capulet and the Nurse have left her, the night before the marriage planned with Paris. The natural impulse is to call them back, to shelter behind them from the trials of life; but she knows they have nothing to offer her, she must rely upon herself; that is the inescapable fact which has been borne in on her bit by bit, ever since she has known Romeo's identity. And one of the essential elements in a portrayal of Juliet which an actress must master in preparation is the gradual realization that nothing will ever be so simple as it has been in her childhood, the gradual admission to herself that she must be prepared to be cut off from everything she has known and be utterly self-sufficient if she is to be able to bestow her frank love on her husband. But of course she knows she cannot be so self-sufficient as to face life with him dead; however much she gives to him because he needs her, she also needs him. And so her doubts of the integrity of the Friar, of the efficacy of the drug, her terror of waking too soon, her sense of guilt for clinging to her love of the man who has killed Tybalt, all vanish before her knowledge of her love for Romeo. Even now, in her utter distress of mind, she is dominated by love for Romeo, by terror for his sake; as much as she fears awakening in the tomb alone and the possibility of going mad and killing herself, she is more horrified at the thought of harm coming to him if he were to make his way to the tomb only to find that, owing to the fears which she has just been expressing, she could not bring herself to drink the drug, and is as a result not there to greet him. Horrified she imagines Tybalt's ghost exacting vengeance from her husband. The thought of Romeo facing

that alone is enough to make her act. With his name on her
lips she drinks:

> Romeo, I come. This do I drink to thee.
>
> (IV, iii, 58)

Again her love for him and her fears for his safety triumph
together over her terror for her own.

Juliet falls asleep with her mind full of Romeo; when she
wakes, her first sight is of the Friar; but her first thought is
of her lord. There is comfort in seeing the Friar, for she
remembers exactly where she ought to be:

> I do remember well where I should be,
> And there I am.

The actress has a small problem here; some may feel that
this line and a half express confidence and satisfaction
that she is where she ought to be; but I myself incline to a
view that Juliet is reminding herself where she is, saying
yes she is where she ought to be, and beginning to wonder
why the Friar and not Romeo is the first person she sees as
she opens her eyes. There is a sense of uneasiness, if no
suspicion of actual disaster; if this view is right, then the
question, 'Where is my Romeo?' comes from increasing
disquiet, from dawning fear that once again something has
thwarted them. Whichever interpretation is chosen, the
objective is the same, desire to be with Romeo; an inability
to be interested in anything in life if he is not included in it.
There seems no need to spend words analysing the obvious
reaction of the girl to the Friar's answer; she merely returns
to the resolution which she made before he gave her the
drug, to kill herself; then it was rather than to betray
Romeo; now it is rather than to live without him. But in
each case the decision comes from that earlier one, made
when she first fell in love with Romeo, that he was the
centre of her life, and from her subsequent determination
to live with no one if she could not live with him. From this

151

position it is not far to a determination not to live without him.

Modern criticism has not only directed attention at the differences between Shakespeare's use of rhetorical figures in his early and his later work; much has been written in a similar vein about his imagery. This is seen to be too poetic and undramatic in the early plays; but unfortunately for the actor, the critic's standard of what is dramatic (valid enough in its own right) has not been formed with any regard to the relation between imagery and the emotional life of the character in whose speeches it occurs. The imagery is interpreted validly as expressing Shakespeare's conception of a theme, an individual, a problem or principle which the play is concerned with, but not as an expression of the character's need, of the emotion which his objective gives rise to in the given situation. Yet the actor's primary concern is with the character; he can serve the long-term purpose of expressing the author's comment, attitude or vision most successfully by acting the character: for Shakespeare has expressed his purpose by means of imagining characters with emotions and desires interacting with one another and with given circumstances. What the literary critic has to say about imagery may well tend to add to an actor's difficulties by quite unintentionally directing his attention away from what will help him to what will hinder him in his task of feeling and wanting truly what the character has been imagined as feeling and wanting. The literary critic may dismiss imagery as decorative and not integrated, and he can stop there; nevertheless what may be defective by the highest standards of dramatic poetry, in that it does not express theme, or might well be spoken by any of the characters, still has to be presented by the actor as if he has no alternative in the circumstances of the play but to use this means of expressing what he must express.

An example of the way in which literary criticism directs attention away from what primarily concerns the actor is afforded us by Professor Clemen's utterly sound and valid comment on some lines spoken by Cassius in *Julius Caesar*:

> Now could I, Casca, name to thee a man
> Most like this dreadful night
> That thunders, lightens, opens graves, and roars
> As doth the lion in the Capitol.
>
> (I, iii, 72–75)

The critic is concerned with 'the harmony between the given situation and the whole atmosphere of the play' which may be traced in the imagery 'by which Shakespeare characterizes his men and women'. The likening of Caesar to the terrifying night is suggested naturally by the 'mood and situation'. For Clemen the image has two functions: 'it characterizes Caesar, and adds to the nocturnal atmosphere'.[1] But this approach ignores what the image does for the character who uses it. Academic literary criticism tends not to ask why must the speaker use this particular image at this moment? The actor must ask and answer this question. Superficially the image seems to be expressing Shakespeare's view of Caesar; but in fact the view given here is not necessarily Shakespeare's but is most certainly Cassius's. Cassius is not afraid of the terrors of this night; therefore his likening of Caesar to the prodigies of the night does not express awe and fear. Cassius likens Caesar to the night because he perceives that there is nothing in the night itself which justifies fear of it; instead the night warns of something else which is abnormal and ought not to be tolerated. For Caesar to become Emperor, Cassius insists, is something abnormal and not to be tolerated: there is no quality in Caesar which makes him the natural person for the office. He points out that the true cause of 'this strange impatience of the heavens' is what the prodigies have been sent to call attention to. For Caesar to rule is as monstrous a state of

[1] W. H. Clemen, *The Development of Shakespeare's Imagery* (1953) pp. 99 f.

abnormality as these prodigies themselves; his rule will
have the same prodigious quality as the night. Cassius does
not fear Caesar, the man, but regards him as trivial and
contemptible; but Caesar, the Emperor, is to be feared.
Here is something which really justifies alarm and
consternation.

In this example there is no quarrel to be had with what
the critic says; the difficulty for the actor consists in what
is left out, and in the suggestion which seems to be
implied that nothing else is to be found there. The critic
may not have intended this implication; it may arise only
in the reader's mind, and the reader alone may be responsible for it. But the fact that such implications may arise and
hamper the actor in his task is what we need to remember.

Even greater difficulty can arise for the actor when the
academic critic denounces imagery as undramatic. Two
images in *Titus Andronicus* have drawn the comment that
they could easily be left out without the text being deprived
thereby of any of its 'comprehensibility and clarity': they
have merely been added to the main sentence after it has
been composed, and not fused simultaneously and organic-
ally with it.[1] The first of these images is spoken by Titus in
a speech expressive of his love and pity as he observes his
mutilated daughter:

> then fresh tears,
> Stood on her cheeks, as doth the honey-dew
> Upon a gath'red lily almost withered.
>
> (III, i, 111–13)

Again the image functions fully only when it is not extracted from the context of the speech; for the function is to
express what Titus feels. He has noticed her tears appearing
on her cheeks when he mentioned her brothers. For him
there is a bitter-sweetness in the sight; the image is evoked
by his overwhelming consciousness of her essential sweet-

---

[1] Clemen, *op. cit.*, pp. 23 f.

ness, of her former beauty before she was despoiled, of the difference between her present state and her former, and of the fact that to those who knew her in full flower of purity and beauty and who still love her there yet remains a trace of what she was, in what she is. The image is an apt expression of this thought and feeling. Whether it was added or not to the main sentence, the actor cannot express the real and sincere feelings of Titus if he leaves the image out. Once he has recognized those feelings by examining the image he will be able to use it to express them.

The second image which has been regarded as not essential to the text comes in the same scene. Lavinia kisses Titus to comfort him when the messenger has entered with two heads and a hand. The sight of her in her pitiable defilement attempting to give consolation prompts Marcus to comment:

> Alas, poor heart, that kiss is comfortless
> As frozen water to a starved snake.
>
> (III, i, 251–2)

The image is very apt and is essential; the comment is deprived of a wealth of meaning, of implication and emotion, if the actor leaves out the second line. Indeed, the first line says very little, and does not express by any means the meaning and emotion of the second. Marcus pities the desolate heart of Titus, which he imagines chilled and drained of warmth; although Lavinia intends her kiss to comfort her father, all it can do is force him to be more than aware of the extent of his miseries, reminding him of what has been done to him and his, thus chilling more instead of thawing the numbness from his heart: this is implied fully and fittingly by the image of the frozen snake ('starved' is used in the sense of 'frozen to death'), whose state can in no wise be remedied by frozen water. There is a strong possibility that Shakespeare is thinking of a frozen snake as one which is hibernating and which could be revived by

155

warmth; then the analogy between Titus' desolate heart and the frozen snake is even more exact. The actor who speaks the two lines can express fully a complexity of implication and emotion for which the first statement—'that kiss is comfortless'—is utterly inadequate.

The fallacy of not asking what images do for the characters who speak them is illustrated again by Clemen's comment on Aaron's lines:[1]

> Now climbeth Tamora Olympus' top,
> Safe out of Fortune's shot, and sits aloft,
> Secure of thunder's crack or lightning flash,
> Advanc'd above pale envy's threat'ning reach.
> As when the golden sun salutes the morn,
> And, having gilt the ocean with his beams,
> Gallops the zodiac in his glistering coach
> And overlooks the highest-peering hills,
> So Tamora.
> Upon her wit doth earthly honour wait,
> And virtue stoops and trembles at her frown.
>
> (II, i, 1–11)

Clemen suggests that lines five to eight, which liken Tamora to the sun, could be left out without the loss of anything important, and even without our noticing it. But these lines add something to what Aaron has said in the first four: the first passage says in effect that Tamora is securely and safely advanced to her pinnacle, invulnerable to Fortune, Heaven's anger and those (presumably mortals) who envy her. Now, having established her state as secure, Aaron proceeds to dwell on its surpassing glory which allows her to feel and be superior to the highest of those beneath her. Against the pallidness of envy (with a possible implication of green in the pallor) Aaron contrasts his vision of a burst of gleaming and golden splendour which is sustained at full height, and is so high above everything on earth, on which it confers

[1] *Op. cit.*, p. 23.

some reflexion of its own glory. 'So Tamora' refers to her splendour as well as her firmly established eminence. In the context of the whole speech the image of the sun is an essential part of Aaron's expression of his objective, which is to make use of Tamora, to let her ruin Rome, but to share all that she has, her wealth, her power, her splendour and her love; for he has her a prisoner in his triumph, 'fetter'd with amorous chains'. Without the image of the sun, whoever acts Aaron cannot express its combination of glory, superiority and contempt for others: all he can say of Tamora is that she is pre-eminent and securely so.

In *Titus Andronicus* such instances of too ready an assumption that the imagery is undramatic are ever to hand. For example, it is advisable not to regard the comparison with Pyramus in the following passage as an undramatic display of learning in a poetic tradition which is irrelevant here. Martius says of Bassianus' body:

> Upon his bloody finger he doth wear
> A precious ring that lightens all this hole,
> Which, like a taper in some monument,
> Doth shine upon the dead man's earthy cheeks,
> And shows the ragged entrails of this pit;
> So pale did shine the moon on Pyramus
> When he by night lay bath'd in maiden blood.
>
> (II, iii, 226–32)

Although the light of the ring has already been compared with a taper, that is no justification for regarding the comparison with the moon as redundant. If the actor knows the the story of Pyramus and Thisbe he will realize that the comparison is exact and is necessary to introduce an element which has not been referred to yet. Pyramus and Thisbe arranged to meet by night under the cover of darkness; but there was just enough light from the moon to reveal the lion that killed Pyramus; the same glimmer of light was

157

enough to let Thisbe see to her horror the blood-stained cloth and her lover's body.

By referring to this story, Martius is able to express the horror of what he is experiencing. Thisbe, like him, was alone with a dead man, in almost total darkness, but with just enough of a glimmer to show not only the dismal sight of the corpse, but more horrifying still, the sickening picture of the surrounding bushes wet with the blood which had spurted from his body as he died. (The myth, after all, explains the existence of the mulberry fruit in this manner.)

The pit has already been described as surrounded by blood-bespattered bushes by Quintus:

> What subtle hole is this,
> Whose mouth is covered with rude-growing briers,
> Upon whose leaves are drops of new-shed blood
> As fresh as morning dew distill'd on flowers?

And in this pit of horror, Martius sees Bassianus as the moon's light revealed Pyramus to Thisbe. What he sees and feels can validly be expressed in terms of her experience; he too, is in darkness, with a pale light making just visible the gruesome sight of the corpse and the red splashes of blood on the bushes all round.

Literary criticism can easily demonstrate that Shakespeare has not used the reference to Pyramus with the skill which he shows in his later work; but the actor is concerned with what relationship there is between the imagery and the emotions of the character he is playing. Once he knows the story, this relation is clear; he can experience the horror of the place and express what he feels so fully that his audience will react as if they too could see, could almost feel the blood in the eery, dim light. They will do this if he does, whether they know the story or not: they are reacting, not to the details of the story of Pyramus, but to his reaction to those details, and to his experience of horror in the pit externalized in his voice (and, if he is visible, in his action).

Again from this same play comes an example to emphasize the point that while the actor ought not to be dead to what literary criticism can have to say about verse-style, he still has to feel sincerely the emotions which the style expresses, even if the expression is inferior in itself to what it might be. The style of the following speech of Tamora is imperfect, but it is not really true to comment in Clemen's words: 'One line is tacked on to the other and the images are added on just as much without preparation as the thoughts.' He is right, however, in declaring that 'the general absence of *enjambement*' results in a pause, so that every line starts off afresh.[1] But the pause is metrical, not emotional; and the fresh start to each line adds not merely another detail to the recital, but gives deeper and more complete expression to the same happiness, and the same objective, which is to make love with the Moor. Tamora is not really talking about the scenery; she uses the scenery to express her own desires, her own elation, her own delight in the thought of lovemaking in this place and at this moment. She wants to make Aaron share her mood and gratify her lust.

> My lovely Aaron, wherefore look'st thou sad
> When everything doth make a gleeful boast?
> The birds chant melody on every bush;
> The snakes lie rolled in the cheerful sun;
> The green leaves quiver with the cooling wind
> And make a chequer'd shadow on the ground;
> Under their sweet shade, Aaron, let us sit.

(II, iii, 10–16)

But Aaron does not respond to her mood as she would like him to. He is not satisfied with the state of things; he has no joy to express; his brooding has nothing to do with love; he contemplates vengeance, he wants blood.

[1] *Op. cit.*, p. 24.

Madam, though Venus govern your desires,
Saturn is dominator over mine.
What signifies my deadly-standing eye,
My silence and my cloudy melancholy,
My fleece of woolly hair that now uncurls
Even as an adder when she doth unroll
To do some fatal execution?
No, madam, these are no venereal signs.
Vengeance is in my heart, death in my hand,
Blood and revenge are hammering in my head.

(II, iii, 30–39)

In this answer there are counterparts to details included in her speech. She speaks of 'melody' he refers to his 'silence'; her 'green leaves' quivering in the 'cooling wind' are opposed by his 'deadly standing eye'; she rejoices in the snakes 'rolled' in the sun, he exults in the menace with which his fleece of woolly hair uncurls like an adder unrolling to strike; and for the 'cheerful sun' in which everything in nature rejoices, he substitutes his 'cloudy melancholy'. Where the happiness of nature can be described as a 'gleeful boast', his appearance expresses a grim purpose which is almost a boast of vengeance.

The existence of these counterparts is not merely a superficial detail of poetic style; they are the result of an interchange of will and emotion between the two characters. Her joy and lust are confronted by his melancholy and hatred, not for her, but for others. But what he wants conflicts with what she does; here is really dramatic writing which allows the players to feel and want truthfully, so that when emotion and desire are externalized in voice and action the characters themselves seem to have come to life. Whatever we may say about the style of these lines they remain essentially dramatic.

Literary criticism quite rightly calls attention to the way in which Shakespeare creates atmosphere through imagery;

but it is dangerous to be persuaded too easily by the literary
critics that in the early plays the images do not grow
naturally out of the situation and the needs of the character.
It has been suggested that the Lieutenant's speech before
the murder of Suffolk is put into the speaker's mouth merely
because the atmosphere is needed, and that the passage has
no special relation to the speaker.[1]

> The gaudy, blabbing, and remorseful day
> Is crept into the bosom of the sea;
> And now loud-howling wolves arouse the jades
> That drag the tragic melancholy night;
> Who with their drowsy, slow, and flagging wings
> Clip dead men's graves, and from their misty jaws
> Breathe foul contagious darkness in the air.
>
> (HENRY VI, PT. II, IV, i, 1–7)

To some extent the comment is valid; these lines could have
been put into the mouths of other characters; but there is
a tone in the passage which fits only those who are ruthless
in bloodshed (of whom, in truth, there are enough in the
play). A careful reading of the sense of the lines, moreover,
reveals an attitude of detached irony which is alien to most
of those who shed blood in this play; they usually delight in
personal malice. The first two lines state that day has sunk
with the sun into the sea. But the speaker sees day as
painting garishly with colours, exposing and betraying, and
then as if in remorse hiding its shame; its remorse is shown
by its creeping away unable to face what it has done. The
word 'jades' expresses more irony in the implied contrast
between the steeds of night and those of the sun. Where the
sun's horses gallop, those of the night drag. Instead of
embracing the air, their wings 'clip' graves; they create
night by the foul darkness they breathe out. Not only are
the horses of night contrasted with those of the sun by

[1]Clemen, pp. 45 f.

implication, but there is an explicit contrast of 'tragic, melancholy night' with the gaudiness of day whose own babbling has created her melancholy. The Lieutenant is revelling in certain aspects of the change from day into night; he is ironically satisfied that after day has made it possible for him to see and capture his prize, it gives way to night, the time of evil most fitted to his purpose with his captives. The images do more than create the atmosphere of nature; they express something which the character is feeling; they say something about the nature of their speaker and his intentions which enables an actor to bring him to life as a character. The ironic ruthlessness, the detachment which is in these lines, emerge again in the Lieutenant's reply to Suffolk's argument that Jove went disguised, as he desperately tries to convince his captors of his identity. 'But Jove was never slain as thou shalt be' sounds the same note of sardonic humour as the images of day and night and the play on words in the earlier speech when the Lieutenant threatens that if his prisoners cannot pay a ransom they shall 'with their blood stain this discoloured shore'.

The actor, then, has to be wary of accepting the literary critic's judgement of a passage as a guide to the way in which the character who speaks it must be played. For the literary critic's approval as well as denunciation does not concern itself with what is vital to acting—the functioning of the image for the character who uses it. So much has been said and written about the success with which Shakespeare dispenses with the need for scenery by his use of imagery that even actors may be so conscious of this function of a passage as to attempt deliberately to create an effect of word-painting as if the character were describing a scene so that others could see it. But usually the character's descriptive imagery involves an emotional reaction to what he is seeing; he has an attitude to it as either helping or obstructing him in attaining his objective. For instance, Romeo and Juliet hardly describe the scene in the garden when she is on the balcony and he below. Her reference to the orchard walls expresses her fear for him, her awareness that he takes risks for her; he refers to the dark as something which hides him; it is because the players feel as if they were there with the high orchard walls between him and safety that the audience imagines the place and the atmosphere of moonlight; Romeo does not describe the moonlight on the trees as one who is trying to paint the picture for others to see it in their minds' eyes; and the actor who tries hard to make the audience see in this way will fail. If, however, the actor imagines the moon—the 'blessed moon'—if he feels it blessed, touching the fruit-tree tops, and feels really what Shakespeare imagined Romeo feeling, then the audience will imagine the scene, even if the stage is bare of scenery. It is the same with the leave-taking; the players will fail if they try to paint the lark, the approach of daylight; they will succeed if they imagine the scene and react to what they have imagined with truthful feeling. Juliet's refusal to accept what she sees as day because she does not want to be parted yet is what matters, not the poetic description of day about to dawn. Romeo's representative will make us see and hear the lark high up in the new-born morning only if he imagines himself looking up at it, and feeling, again truthfully and really, the imagined Romeo's emotions—his readiness to die, his reckless determination to take the consequences if she would prefer him to stay longer and not leave now.

When the actor asks why he as the character must use a particular image, he ought not to be satisfied with the answer that the image is important to the expressing of Shakespeare's theme, or of his attitude to some point at issue: such answers are not to be ignored, but they should not be accepted as adequate. For instance, it is a commonplace of academic Shakespeare criticism that Macbeth has been imagined as one who attempts to occupy a place which he does not fit, and that this is expressed in terms of images involving clothes which are too big or owned by somebody else or which are uncomfortable in their unfamiliarity. Without disputing the validity of such observations, we must remember that they do not help an actor in his main task of creating the character. When Macbeth asks 'Why do you dress me in borrowed robes?' he is not merely thinking of himself as somebody given something which is not his; he is not just asking for information. He is startled; it is as if someone else as well as the witches has spoken his secret thoughts aloud; the question is among other things an attempt to protect himself by disclaiming higher positions which belong rightfully to other people.

In the same way, concentration on the images of darkness in this play as functioning chiefly as an expression of Shakespeare's conception of evil, as a reaction to his own imagining of evil overwhelming Scotland, will not help to relate the individual images to the emotional life of the character who speaks them. When Macbeth uses images of darkness they express for him a need to be protected against everything in Creation that is opposed to him and his 'black and deep desires'. His invocation to the stars to hide their fires expresses a fear of what will happen if his longings are exposed. This is before the murder; after it, he looks on night and darkness as a protection against the consequences of his deed. He has come to associate Banquo with the 'bloody instructions' which he himself has taught; through Banquo's hand, he fears, they will return to plague the inventor. And so he invokes night.

> Come, seeling night,
> Scarf up the tender eye of pitiful day.
> (III, iii, 46–47)

To seel is to sew up the eyelids of a hawk before hoodwinking it; the hoodwinking itself is done by means of a bandage which is tied round the bird's eyes so that they will not be damaged by responding to light with a reflex action which will tear the tender lids. The bandage is known as a scarf; it is to be seen in traditional paintings and drawings of Cupid, Fortune and Justice, all of whom have a bandage, or scarf, tied round their eyes. The terms 'hoodwink' and 'scarf' occur in this sense in Benvolio's 'We'll have no Cupid hoodwink'd with a scarf' (ROMEO AND JULIET, I, iv, 4). Night is conceived of by Macbeth as a falconer who 'scarfs up' (that is, hoodwinks by means of a bandage) the tender eyes of the hawk, 'pitiful day'. But the bird in terms of whose scarfing-up the image functions is by no means pitiful; it is actually devoid of pity. Nevertheless, to Macbeth day, light and pity are all enemies to whom he fears to be exposed. The image expresses a terror of being perceived by something above which, when it sees him, will pounce on him, dropping out of the sky like a hawk on its prey. He uses the image because it can carry the exact quality of his terror, of his sense of exposure perpetually to punishment for what he has done, and to the obstructing of what he proposes to do.

What has evoked much admiration and much valuable comment from literary critics of this play is Shakespeare's expression of his conception of evil, and the way evil oppresses Scotland, in the imagery of Lady Macbeth's invocation to night.

> Come, thick night,
> And pall thee in the dunnest smoke of hell,
> That my keen knife see not the wound it makes,
> Nor heaven peep through the blanket of the dark
> To cry, 'Hold, hold'.
>
> (I, v, 47–51)

Her principal desire is that she shall not be prevented from committing the murder; she does not think further than that, certain that success there is success everywhere. The surface sense of her lines is an invocation to thick night to

165

come, covered in the darkest smoke of hell so that her keen knife shall not see the wound it is engaged in making, and so that the covering of the dark will be too thick to allow heaven to peep through it to cry, 'Stop, stop.' From this sense we are given the implications that she wants a darkness so intense that if her sharp knife were able to see ('keen' seems to suggest 'keen-sighted') it would not be able to perceive the wound which it is actually making, close as the two are together; there is also the implication that the wound is such that the knife might turn in her hand against what it is being used for. The image of heaven peeping through the cover of darkness expresses Lady Macbeth's awareness of the unnaturalness of what she proposes to do, of the extreme unlikeliness that she will be allowed to do it, and of the intensity of her resolution to do it nonetheless, even at the cost of dedicating herself to evil. The hyperbolic quality of the whole passage derives from the knowledge, packed deeply away beneath the conscious mind, that really she cannot succeed in the long run. But her conscious mind is concerned only with murdering Duncan; all it wants is not to be prevented by heaven from murdering the King. Here she differs from her husband, whose conscious mind recognizes the impossibility of ultimate success, and the fact that Duncan's 'surcease' will not necessarily bring it.

This is the topic with which Macbeth is concerned in his soliloquy which begins with the words, 'If it were done'. His first statement is constructed in three sets of equivalents: 'if'—'when'—'then'; 'it were'—''tis'—''twere'—'It were'; 'done'—'done'—'done'; and the sense of this structure is that if it were really done with when it is done then it would be a good idea to act swiftly.

> If it were done when 'tis done, then 'twere well
> It were done quickly.

The implications arising from this sense are, first, a realization that he is seeing more clearly than his wife, who shares his wish to kill Duncan, but not his fear that the mere killing of Duncan will not bring what the murderer wants. For what Macbeth wants—his objective—is to enjoy all that Duncan enjoys, which involves the certainty that there will be no enjoyment of what he wants to steal from the King unless he feels safe from the consequences. This comes out clearly and explicitly in the next statement:

> If th' assassination
> Could trammel up the consequence, and catch
> With his surcease, success.

And here the sense is expressed in a structure which involves the antithetical 'assassination'—'consequence', the equivalents, 'trammel up'—'catch', the paranomasia, 'surcease'—'success'; there is also the connexion of 'trammel up the consequences' with 'catch success'. 'Trammel' is used in two senses; one, 'to catch in a net', the other, as a verb derived from the noun used of the tasselled cords for tying a shroud round the feet of a corpse. Macbeth is saying, 'If killing Duncan could catch the consequences of the deed in a net at the same time as his death caught success'; and there is the implication that he would also like the assassination to tie up all the unpleasant consequences for the murderer in the shroud with the body of his victim.

The mere assassination of Duncan will not achieve Macbeth's objective and he knows it:

> that but this blow
> Might be the be-all and the end-all here—
> But here upon this bank and shoal of time—
> We'd jump the life to come.

The intensity of his need is expressed in the structure 'but this blow'—'the be-all and the end-all here'; 'might be'—'we'd jump'; 'bank and shoal'—'the life to come'. If this single blow were enough to put an end to the matter in this life (this sandbank of time), we would risk what might

167

happen in the life to come. As Macbeth has been described somewhat misleadingly as spiritually blind, the actor should notice here the clarity of his vision: the image, 'this bank and shoal of time', expresses perfectly the knowledge that what is permanent in this life is in fact only transitory; a sandbank seems stable and permanent compared with flux of water around it; and this life seems a solid moment in the sea of time; but neither is really permanent. Yet for such transitory and illusory permanence Macbeth is ready to risk what will happen to him in the eternal permanence of the life after death. He is perturbed only by what might happen to him in this life as a result of assassinating Duncan. But it is what might happen in this life that actually makes him pause (Hamlet is perturbed about the life to come).

> But in these cases
> We still have judgement here.

But in cases such as this we always have our judgement, our case is always tried and judgement pronounced 'here', not in 'the life to come'.

> that we but teach
> Bloody instructions, which being taught return
> To plague th' inventor.

And the sentence takes the form of punishing the sinner by means of his own sin, in a case like this by his being murdered as the result of his own success having suggested to somebody else that he might be disposed of in the same fashion.

> This even-handed justice
> Commends th' ingredience of our poison'd chalice
> To our own lips.

The sense of this is clearer if we remember that 'commends' means 'bestows' as well as 'recommends', and 'ingredience' is 'the mixture'. Once again Macbeth is recognizing that he must expect an impartial judgement which will use his own sin to punish him. There is a fearful admission of the irony that punishment should come in this way, which amounts almost to unwilling admiration of a principle of justice whose practice must restrain or crush him.

Macbeth now considers the case that would be brought against him at this judgement 'here'. Two things will speak in witness against him, for he would be breaking a double trust: the first of these consists in a breach of the bond of being both kinsman and subject, both of which will be strong against the deed at the judgement as they ought to be in deterring him from the murder; but if they are weak as deterrents in themselves, they are strong inasmuch as their voices will carry weight at his trial. The second point which will speak against him will be that his duty as host is to protect Duncan, not murder him; the foulness of the murder is intensified by the misuse of hospitality. Here the actor is helped by Shakespeare's structure of antithesis which connects 'host' with 'murderer' and 'shut the door' with 'bear the knife myself'.

> He's here in double trust:
> First, as I am his kinsman and his subject—
> Strong both against the deed; then as his host,
> Who should against his murderer shut the door,
> Not bear the knife myself.

If Macbeth were brought to judgement for the murder of Duncan, not only would his sins speak against him, but he would be, equally if not more, discredited by Duncan's virtues pleading for Duncan. 'Even-handed justice' does not judge the sinner alone; it dispenses rewards as well as punishments; it will reward Duncan as well as punish Macbeth. And the saving of Duncan, like the punishing of Macbeth, involves a judgement which does not wait until Doomsday, when Gabriel's trumpet will summon the dead. Now the trumpet-tongued virtues of Duncan, pleading against Macbeth's deed, pleading for Duncan not to be judged when murdered in his sleep—exposed then to sin, although his life has been so virtuous—will speak against Macbeth and encompass his undoing by awakening the very element of pity in the universe, so that the supernatural and terrifying messenger of heaven will uncover his crimes to the eyes of humanity; and once that has happened he cannot last long. Although this vision of judgement, punishing him and rewarding Duncan, is expressed in rich and complex imagery, Macbeth's thought-processes are by no means obscure. He has been saying he is afraid that to murder Duncan will bring him a fitting judgement in this life: he enumerates the aspects of the crime which will tell most heavily against him at the judging: and then he sees that even more certain to encompass his downfall is the fact that by advancing his judgement from Doomsday to this life, he will also be advancing Duncan's judgement from Doomsday until the moment of his murder. And the fact that Duncan must be saved from his danger by the voice of his virtues means that Macbeth will be shown doubly culpable. The quality of the crime against Duncan and justice is bound up with the quality of Duncan himself: to do this to any king were bad enough, but to a man like Duncan it is far worse. Similarly, the vengeance of Heaven will be enlisted for any king, but in Duncan's cause it will be far more terrible and swift. The witnesses that speak against Macbeth will combine against him with those that speak in favour of his victim. Justice done to Duncan will make doubly certain that justice is done to his murderer; and it will take the form he fears most, of exposure to the consequences of the crime. These, I believe, are the ideas and emotions expressed in the images whose surface sense has already been discussed (see Chapter Three, pp. 78ff.):

> Besides, this Duncan
> Hath borne his faculties so meek, hath been

So clear in his great office, that his virtues
Will plead like angels, trumpet-tongu'd, against
The deep damnation of his taking-off;
And pity, like a naked new-born babe,
Striding the blast, or heaven's cherubin hors'd
Upon the sightless couriers of the air,
Shall blow the horrid deed in every eye,
That tears shall drown the wind.

The result of this outburst of terror that to commit this murder will have these consequences is that Macbeth ends the soliloquy in exactly the same position as when he started it. His objective has always been to enjoy what Duncan enjoys, which presupposes Duncan's tranquillity of mind, and the certainty that 'if it were done' it really were done with. Knowing clearly that he cannot expect to escape the consequences on which he dwells because he sees clearly the quality of the crime he is pondering, Macbeth finds himself still unable to decide quickly to act, and to act quickly having made the decision, and he is still equally unable to put from his heart his longing to get rid of Duncan and inherit all that rightfully belongs to such a king.

I have no spur
To prick the sides of my intent, but only
Vaulting ambition, which o'er-leaps itself,
And falls on th' other.

He is envisaging his resolution ('intent') as a horse which will not jump without a spur. He regrets the fact that while he has no spur to make the horse jump, its rider, 'ambition', does not wait for the steed but leaps over the obstacle itself. The word 'vaulting' was used in Shakespeare's day of a rider who took his horse as far as the obstacle and then performed the feat of leaping over it from the saddle himself, leaving the horse behind: but when ambition does this it is not successful. 'Falls on th' other' may mean 'falls on

171

the other side' or, as is much less likely, 'falls on the other' (i.e. on intent). As, however, Macbeth says that ambition 'o'erleaps itself' it is hardly likely that he imagines the rider falling back on the horse without springing over; yet this is possible, as 'o'erleaps itself' may mean 'undoes itself by leaping too much'. In any case, whichever of these interpretations is adopted, it is certain that Macbeth deplores the fact that all his longing, and his fantasies of killing the king, will come to nothing so long as he cannot resolve to act.

He cannot make himself decide to murder Duncan; but he has fantasies in which he is always murdering Duncan. But to turn fantasy into actuality, to do the deed which we can imagine ourselves doing easily enough, requires resolution; and he cannot resolve to act when there is a possibility of being punished in the way which he fears. He still wants Duncan murdered, however, but he wants it done with the certainty that there would be no repercussions. He is neither able to make himself act, nor able to stop himself imagining the deed done with the results which he wants from it.

Part of this soliloquy is often interpreted as expressing the conflict between Macbeth's repugnance to wrongdoing and his sinful desire to gain what can only be gained by wrongdoing. His references to Duncan are interpreted as a sign of his not being utterly depraved, of his capacity to recognize good, to admire it, and to deplore the ambition which he cannot suppress, and which he is just managing to hold in check. While I can see how this view of Macbeth's words can be obtained, I cannot find any real remorse or wish to restrain his ambition because it is evil. Macbeth does not weigh good against evil as such; he balances success against failure; and as he cannot be assured of the success he wants he will not resolve to act. As for recognizing Duncan's virtues, Macbeth certainly does that. But it is because he recognizes these virtues that he finds Duncan a man to be envied. The ambition which the thane cherishes is not merely to be king, but to receive as king everything that he envies in Duncan. He wants to be thought of and loved as well as obeyed as Duncan is: this becomes clear to us moderns as the action progresses, but there is every probability that the Jacobean mind associated the real allegiance of spirit, the love and admiration paid to a fine monarch, so closely with possession of the crown that one implied the other.

One thing must strike the modern mind, too, however; from the beginning of the play, certainly almost from the very moment of his first entrance into the action, Macbeth shows himself a man who can be thoroughly frightened. Whatever may be said of his fearlessness by others and of his disdain of Fortune, he shows fear and he asks to know what the future holds for him. When the witches hail Macbeth as one 'that shalt be King hereafter', his reaction is described by Banquo's question:

> Good sir, why do you start, and seem to fear
> Things that do sound so fair?
>
> (I, iii, 51–52)

Macbeth must have started, that is jerked violently, in fear; his appearance is of someone who is afraid of what he has heard. The fear itself which the actor has to feel is associated with his vision of the murder 'as yet phantastical' which is his automatic response to the greeting; there is also the strong possibility that he may be terrified by hearing his own deep longings put into words by these supernatural creatures. Obviously the two sources of fear are not incompatible.

Macbeth recognizes that his fear affects him through his imagination. Even in this early part of the play Macbeth longs for Duncan's crown while he is frightened by the imagining of what he must do to get it. He indignantly repudiates Banquo's warning against letting himself be won by the instruments of darkness with honest trifles, and

173

insists to himself that these truths are not what Banquo suggests: these two truths, he asserts, because he wants to think it,

>   are told
> As happy prologues to the swelling act
> Of the imperial theme.

He is committed in his heart to a longing for the throne of Scotland, and is inclined to receive with welcome any assurance that he will be king, whatever the source. And so he is sure that the incitement by the witches cannot be evil; but at the moment that he thinks this, he is struck by the opposite thought—it cannot be good.

>   This supernatural soliciting
>   Cannot be ill;

and now, hot on the heels of assurance, comes a doubt,

>   Cannot be good.

Now debating the problem, trying to come to a certainty, he tells himself that what he has heard so far has been confirmed, 'I am Thane of Cawdor'. On the other hand, he recognizes that there must be something wrong with a greeting which has such an effect on him physically through the strength of the image it evokes in his imagination. The suggestion that he might be king releases a longing expressed in so vivid an imagining of Duncan murdered as to make his hair stand on end and make his heart thud alarmingly and unnaturally. He decides that to be face to face with what is dreaded is less than to be disturbed by horrible imaginings. And this horrible imagining, he tells us, is so strong as to be an hallucination; yet as we have seen in Chapter Three (pp. 75f.), although he knows he is imagining the murder and can distinguish between the hallucination and reality, he has been affected so powerfully that he continues to react to 'what is not' as if it were real. At this

174

point in the action Macbeth has hopes that he can avoid doing what terrifies him, and still be king:

> If chance will have me king, why, chance may crown
>   me
> Without my stir.

And he adds that let come whatever may, the roughest day eventually comes to an end as time and the hour runs through it.

But when Macbeth hears Duncan name Malcolm as the next King of Scotland he knows that chance will not have him king without his stir.

> The Prince of Cumberland! That is a step,
> On which I must fall down, or else o'er-leap,
> For in my way it lies.

At this point he considers the source of his fear for the first time since entering the action of the play. He fears being known for what he is, a man who seems loyal, but who harbours 'black and deep desires'. They must not come to light; if they do he will not be able to kill Duncan; or even if he were to manage that, exposure of his true nature will alienate all over whom he comes to rule; to keep the throne against all comers in these circumstances would be futile, for he wants to reign without being known for what he really is. Macbeth is longing to do the deed, is afraid of doing it, yet is utterly committed to wanting it done.

> Stars, hide your fires;
> Let not light see my black and deep desires.
> The eye wink at the hand; yet let that be
> Which the eye fears, when it is done, to see.
>
> (I, iv, 48–53)

The imagery of these lines expresses a desire to be hidden by darkness, not merely against men, but from the sight of God; Macbeth is aware of the fundamental conflict between

175

his desires for the throne and everything associated with light, with the fires of heaven, both literally and metaphorically. And underneath the longing to be thus hidden there lies a conviction, even deeper than his 'black and deep desires', that he cannot be successful so long as wrong is not right.

Fear of failure is still strong enough in Macbeth when he meets his wife to prevent him committing himself to immediate action. He refuses to be drawn into argument at the moment, but what he wants and what he fears can be read clearly in his face. And despite her exhorting him to 'look up clear' and leave the rest to her, he has decided to do nothing, or rather he has not decided to do anything that night.

When she comes after him, just as his soliloquy finishes with the image of the horse whose rider vaults himself, he greets her with an attempt at decisiveness, 'We will proceed no further in this business.' The reason which he gives seems conclusive enough, but it is actually based on a logical fallacy.

> He hath honour'd me of late; and I have bought
> Golden opinions from all sorts of people,
> Which would be worn now in their newest gloss,
> Not cast aside so soon.

If Macbeth were really talking about clothes the logic would be flawless. It is good sense and good economics to wear clothes in 'their newest gloss' before casting them off as outworn. But he is not talking about clothes; he is actually talking about the 'golden opinions' which he has bought. And in outgrowing his present stature he does not make himself too great for the golden opinions of those who honour him as he is now. These would become even more golden, they would not be lost unused; the admiration attached to the new Thane of Cawdor will still be attached to the new King of Scotland. But the way in which Macbeth expresses himself betrays his conviction that to become King by murdering Duncan would necessarily lead to the loss of the golden opinions which are now his. He does not believe that he can attain the success that he wants. He is not like Tamburlaine and Richard, Duke of Gloucester. 'Is it not brave to be a king,' Tamburlaine asks, 'Is it not passing brave to be a king?' For him 'the ripest fruit of all' is

> That perfect bliss and sole felicity,
> The sweet fruition of an earthly crown.

And Richard exhorts his father,
> do but think
> How sweet a thing it is to wear a crown,
> Within whose circuit is Elysium
> And all that poets feign of bliss and joy.

But Macbeth wants the crown for something which in itself is not difficult to sympathize with; not for power, not for pomp and glory as ends in themselves. When he has lost all hope of ever having what he did the murder for, he recognizes that although he is safe (the witches have convinced him that he is),

> that which should accompany old age,
> As honour, love, obedience, troops of friends,
> I must not look to have.
> (v, iii, 24–26)

In these lines Macbeth sums up what he wants out of life, the 'honour, love, obedience, troops of friends' such as only a king could have, only a king of the calibre of Duncan.

Because she knows this, Lady Macbeth is able to brush away easily his insistence that he wants to enjoy what he has already acquired instead of spurning it for something better. He is indeed afraid to be the 'the same' in his 'act and valour' as he is 'in desire'; he has admitted that to himself before she came to him. For that reason the taunt does not move him, nor does her logical argument that without what he really wants, the honour and loyalty given to Duncan, he would not be satisfied with anything less, because satisfaction would always be cancelled by his own knowledge of himself as a coward.

Macbeth's answer to this is the declaration, which is strictly true, that he dare do all that does become a man, and 'Who dares do more is none.' Whatever indignation he may raise, true or false, he knows, of course, that she is right, he is afraid; but it is because he is afraid that all her fire cannot incite him. Instead, it draws from him the reason which really stops him acting, and which he has never hidden from himself; he is afraid of failure. Rather than fail he would go on in the present state, with his fantasies of murdering Duncan and his inability to bring himself to decide actually to commit the murder. She can deal with this; first she has torn down his feeble pretence that he would be satisfied with what he has as Thane of Cawdor, so that his desire for all that goes with the throne of Scotland shall exert its full force; and now she sweeps aside his fear of failure with what looks like a foolproof plan. So far as committing the murder is concerned and seizing the throne, the plan is foolproof. But until this moment Macbeth has seen clearly that no plan can be successful for him unless it can circumvent the consequences of judgement in this life as well. The important point for the actor at this moment, therefore, is what happens to the character so that he decides, despite the better knowledge he has shown, to commit himself to action. It seems to me that he is subjected to an intolerable tension from the moment he leaves Duncan to prepare his wife for the King's coming. The fact that the opportunity has made itself for him, that it will not last long, that once gone it may never return, increases the fever of his desire to assassinate the King. He resents his inability to be resolute, not his inability to dismiss his evil longings from his heart. He would like to be convinced that he can act in

178

safety and that he can evade judgement 'here'. Lady Macbeth has never considered that success involves more than killing Duncan secretly and seizing his throne. She does not make her husband want it more; but she prevents him from deceiving himself into thinking that he wants it less than he does; and then her fiery confidence tips the balance, so that he believes what he has wanted to believe, that Duncan's 'surcease' can catch 'success' for his murderer. Macbeth has never been restrained by his knowledge that what he contemplates is evil; he has been concerned only with his chances of success or failure. Once persuaded of success, momentarily, there is nothing to restrain his desires; now his fantasy can become actual; the horse jumps under its rider; intent supports ambition.

Lady Macbeth has not only counselled swift and ruthless action: she has also argued that deceit is necessary for the success of their plans. What she suggests combines ruthlessness with deception, evoking in him not only admiration for her 'undaunted mettle' but delight in the deception itself:

> Will it not be receiv'd,
> When we have mark'd with blood those sleepy two
> Of his own chamber, and us'd their very daggers,
> That they have done 't?
>
> (I, vii, 74–77)

The delight here is centred on the thought 'of his own chamber' and of using 'their very daggers'. He is an apt pupil. In their earlier interview, Lady Macbeth urged on him the importance of not letting his thoughts be read on his face, of playing the white devil and showing in his appearance the very opposite of the black and deep desires which he is himself afraid of coming to light. He has learnt to look like the innocent flower and 'be the serpent under it'. Now, utterly resolute, he is ready to make every mental and physical effort to do the deed; and he delights at the

same time in the way in which he will 'beguile the time':
he is prepared both to be ruthless and to seem innocent and
pitifully distressed by what he himself will do:

> I am settled, and bend up
> Each corporal agent to this terrible feat.
> Away, and mock the time with fairest show;
> False face must hide what the false heart doth know.
>
> (I, vii, 79–82)

Once more, the intensity of Macbeth's imagining brings
on hallucination; thinking of the dagger which he will use
against Duncan, he finds himself apparently seeing it, and
his desire to use 'such an instrument' is enough to make
him imagine the visionary dagger running with blood. The
vision is an expression of his preparedness for the deed; it
does not frighten him; he reaches for it eagerly because,
above all, he intends to use it. Then only is he sure that it
is a vision and not a real dagger: yet it may be something
which has materialized thanks to supernatural intervention
exactly when he needs it; then it would be 'sensible to
feeling' as well as to sight. Or, as he recognizes, it may not
be something created outside him for his use, but 'a dagger
of the mind', an illusion, 'a false creation' of his own fevered
mind. All this time his purpose never wavers; the dagger
still looks as if it could be felt as well as seen, and it marshals
him in the direction in which he was going in any case. He
feels it must be a material dagger not an illusion; his eyes
alone insist it is there, perhaps because the other senses let
them be duped, or because they are more accurate than the
other senses, and are alone capable of responding to what
really is there. Then, when he has seen gouts of blood on it,
he realizes 'there's no such thing', that his concentration on
what he is going to do has led his eyes to see what he is
imagining. If anything, more resolute, Macbeth now celebrates the 'witching-hour of night' as Hamlet calls it; a time
utterly suited to the deed to which he is dedicating himself.

There is still a hint of fear that his secrecy will be disturbed, that the slightest sound of a footstep will be heard and thus 'take the present horror from the time' in two senses; first, the sound of a human footstep will literally break the horrifying silence which follows on the cry of the wolf; and second, even the slightest footfall may awaken some sleeper, obstruct the plan which will have to be relinquished at the very moment most fitted to it. Each of these senses expresses Macbeth's longing to kill Duncan and his fear of exposure. But as nothing occurs to deter him, after a wry laugh at himself for speaking while Duncan still lives, the determined murderer says resolutely:

> I go and it is done.

As soon as Duncan is dead, Macbeth finds himself really in the position in which he has so often and so intensely imagined himself; now guilty of murder in deed and therefore open to 'judgement here'. So long as his murder was only in thought, his guilt would be judged after death; but he is terrified of what might happen to him here. His conscience does not torment him with fears of judgement in the life to come; his reason is not terrified with the thought of damnation; if that happened there would be a possibility of contrition, of changing his ways. But he never turns back; indeed, at one possible turning-point, after the vision of Banquo's ghost has made him betray his guilt to his subjects, he asserts:

> I am in blood
> Stepp'd in so far that, should I wade no more,
> Returning were as tedious as go o'er.
>
> (III, iv, 136–8)

As his conscience cannot touch his reason, it can only affect the irrational part of him, his senses; they are prevailed on through the imagination to hear and see terrifying sounds and sights. There is the voice crying 'sleep no more' which embodies for him his knowledge that he will never sleep soundly again so long as he is tortured with fears of the earthly consequences of his 'bloody instructions'. Not only the imaginary voice, but the actual knocking can appal him; he knows it is a knocking, but it sounds like something terrifying and supernatural, an externalization of the terror he feels at the thought of what he has done to himself by what he has done to Duncan. The scene immediately after the murder shows him completely shattered by the knowledge that his guilt can never be cleansed and by the conviction that it can never be hidden; that the mere attempt to remove its signs will necessarily end in its being all the more obvious.

It is possible to interpret Macbeth's 'Wake Duncan with thy knocking, I would thou couldst!' as sincere remorse for Duncan's murder. I think, however, that he is still concerned with himself; he would like Duncan alive that he himself might not be exposed to the horrible dangers which are the result of what he has done. As one seventeenth-century writer puts it, 'Consciences that are without remorse are not without horror: wickedness makes men desperate.'[1] And horror is what Macbeth has in his conscience, tormenting him with visions, with sounds, with terrible dreams, but unable to move him one step towards repentance. He wishes he had not done the deed because its consequences are so terrifying, not because the deed itself was wrong.

Once crowned, Macbeth experiences 'horrible imaginings' just as he knew he would before the murder. The situation is summed up wonderfully in the soliloquy expressing his fears and hatred of Banquo.

> To be thus is nothing,
> But to be safely thus.

[1] J. Hall, *Contemplations, Cain and Abel, Works*, ed. P. Hall (1838–9), I, 18.

182

His objective has always embraced not only being king, but enjoying kingship in safety. Without safety kingship is nothing, for until he feels safe he will be tormented by fears. Quite naturally the fears centre on Banquo, who knows all about the witches, and who was hailed as father to a line of kings; there is no one more likely to have learnt Macbeth's bloody instructions and to be ready to profit by them. And so Banquo and his son must die, to free Macbeth from 'these terrible dreams/That shake us nightly'. In the torture of the fears which come from his guilty conscience Macbeth can envy Duncan his sound sleep in the grave. The usurper lives and wakes to fear treason, steel, poison, malice domestic, foreign levy: they all play their part as possible means of judgement on him.

Macbeth still combines deceit with ruthlessness; the murder must be done in secret and 'something from the palace', and though he could sweep Banquo away with 'bare-faced power', bare is the last thing he must let his face be since Duncan's murder; he must live in public in a visor, using his face to express the opposite of his intentions. Thus there was the false courteousness to Banquo at his leave-taking, and the admonition to Lady Macbeth (to hide his plans even from her) to show special favour to the man marked down as a victim, who will be dead before the favour can be shown. However bitterly Macbeth regrets laving 'our honours in these flattering streams' he must do it, because for a while anything else is unsafe for him.

As a result of deceit and ruthlessness there is one moment when Macbeth feels he has attained his objective; that is when he hears that Banquo is dead; but the moment is all too short; disillusionment and terrible disappointment, with all the old fears crowding in on them, come when he is told that Fleance escaped. And so once more he is tormented by the fears whose source he so accurately analysed in his ruminations just before his wife persuaded him, against his better knowledge, with her 'we'll not fail'. But ruthlessness has failed, so he falls back on deceit to save him now. He must seem innocent, he must already prepare to meet the accusation of whose accuracy he is all too conscious; he must seem surprised and disappointed at Banquo's absence. But to think of Banquo, for Macbeth, with his imagination and with his guilty conscience, is to see what he fears, and what he wants to keep hidden. When Macbeth imagines something intensely enough, he sees it; he is thinking of the dead Banquo, afraid of his guilt being discovered, anticipating his need to show his utter innocence and ignorance of the murder; but above all, there is in his mind the thought of Banquo 'with twenty trenched gashes on his head', and so he sees what he is thinking of as if it really were before him. Thinking intensely of using his dagger brought him a vision of a dagger, the exact replica of the one, his own, that was in his mind, and with such apparent reality that its shape looked 'as palpable as' the real dagger which he drew from its sheath. Now thinking intensely of the dead Banquo with his hideous wounds on his head, Macbeth is confronted with what looks like the actual body of his victim as he has imagined it. In the split second before he assumes he is looking at Banquo's ghost his reaction is an assumption of innocence expressed as a stern demand of his courtiers, 'Which of you have done this?' At this his own guilty conscience makes the apparition accuse him. His denial, 'Thou canst not say I did it' is contradicted by his own knowledge, which makes him imagine the vision nodding its head at him as if to say, 'yes, I can'. This brings from him 'never shake/Thy gory locks at me'.

It is usual to assume that what Macbeth sees is Banquo's ghost, which reveals itself to the murderer and to nobody else present. I am suggesting, however, that what he sees is the same kind of vision as the dagger, something proceeding from his 'heat-oppressed brain'. For, when the episode is over, he recognizes that what has happened to him has been

deception of himself, that he persuaded himself of the truth
of an illusion.

> My strange and self-abuse
> Is the initiate fear that wants hard use.

'Abuse' is used in the sense of 'deception'; the lines mean
that his strange deception practised on himself is the result
of a beginner's fear, or of a fear which is itself only a
beginner, and which has not been used much, nor become
accustomed to stern practices.

My suggestion that the apparition should be interpreted
in this way is not only supported by this speech, but makes
sense psychologically of the appearances and disappearances
of the vision. It first appears when Macbeth is anxious to
prove his innocence before it is impugned. When he masters
his fear with 'Why, what care I? If thou canst nod, speak,
too', it is because he thinks that instead of horrible imaginings of how appalling it would be if Banquo could come
when he is 'challenged for unkindness' he is confronted with
the 'present fear'. And as Macbeth can face the present fear
it no longer dominates him; so with its disappearance from
his mind, the vision disappears from his sight. But when he
has to show his innocence again by drinking to Banquo and
sighing, 'would he were here', he overplays his hand. While
he speaks the words he thinks again how terrifying it would
be if the dead Banquo were there, and again the vision takes
shape before his eyes. This time, as well, it disappears when
Macbeth overcomes his fear. It is clear that what unnerves
Macbeth is the form the vision takes, the dead Banquo as he
imagines him mutilated by his wounds. But when the
murderer gets to the point of dominating his terrors by
commanding the vision to disappear, calling it what it is, a
shadow, an unsubstantial appearance, an unreal mockery,
then it quite naturally troubles his sight no longer. But
Macbeth himself still thinks that everybody has seen what
he has seen, and marvels in particular that his wife could

'keep the natural ruby' of her cheeks when his were 'blanch'd with fear'.

By the time that his guests have departed Macbeth is convinced that he, together with 'the secret'st man of blood', cannot hope to keep his crimes hidden. He is now no longer concerned to hide his guilt; there is no longer any point in it. Now he concentrates on the other of the two means which his wife counselled him to use; he will employ ruthlessness. He decides to carve out safety for himself at no matter what cost to others; and still terrified of the form which his 'judgement here' may take, he resolves 'to know/ By the worst means the worst'. Determined that for his own good 'all causes shall give way', he now expresses his despair in the image of wading through blood which has already been considered (see p. 181).

The intensity of Macbeth's fear, and of his objective, to enjoy the throne in safety, is expressed by the violence of his conjuration of the witches, when he is prepared for all Creation to be destroyed, merely so that he shall be liberated from uncertainty. Just as he wanted to believe that he could succeed in his enterprise against Duncan, so now he wants to believe that there is no need to fear judgement in this life, that he will not be punished by meeting premature death at the hands of an opponent. As his will to be persuaded led him to accept his wife's assurances on the former occasion, so now he swallows greedily the reassurance served to him by the witches at his own request.

The episode with the witches frees Macbeth of fear completely; nothing can now restrain him from acts of ruthlessness; there is no need to dissemble, there is no need to fear vengeance, he is certain of his own invulnerability. But it is now that he experiences his most bitter disillusioning; to be 'thus' was nothing when he was not safe. But now, thinking himself safe, he finds that he is no longer 'thus'— he is no longer an honoured monarch, admired, praised and served gratefully and willingly with the 'service and the loyalty' which they owe and which 'in doing it, pays itself'. Instead he is hated; as Caithness puts it:

> Those he commands move only in command,
> Nothing in love.
>
> (v, ii, 19–20)

Macbeth's false sense of security keeps him free from fears of judgement in this life. Waiting to hear what the wailing of the women is about, confident of his castle's strength, he congratulates himself on the change in him which leaves him literally fearless:

> I have almost forgot the taste of fears.
> The time has been my senses would have cool'd
> To hear a night-shriek, and my fell of hair
> Would at a dismal treatise rouse and stir
> As life were in't. I have supp'd full with horrors;
> Direness, familiar to my slaughterous thoughts,
> Cannot once start me.
>
> (v, v, 9–15)

He has already acknowledged to himself the reason for this lack of fear; when told of defections from his forces, his reply was:

> Bring me no more reports; let them fly all.
> Till Birnam Wood remove to Dunsinane
> I cannot taint with fear. What's the boy Malcolm?
> Was he not born of woman? The spirits that know
> All mortal consequences have pronounc'd me thus:
> 'Fear not, Macbeth; no man that's born of woman
> Shall e'er have power upon thee.'
>
> (v, iii, 1–7)

It followed that he was not perturbed by reports of false thanes going over to the English: so long as he has confidence in the truth of the spirits' assurances it is true of Macbeth that:

187

The mind I sway by and the heart I bear
Shall never sag with doubt nor shake with fear.

(v, iii, 9–10)

It follows, too, that, when he hears the news of Birnam Wood moving, his fear should sap his resolution, and he should begin to doubt (in the sense of 'fear' as well as the modern 'lack confidence in')

th' equivocation of the fiend
That lies like truth.

(v, v, 43–44)

But his despair does not disarm him completely: like many desperate men, heroes and criminals, he resolves to fight it out. After Malcolm's attack has been launched, Macbeth fights desperately, tormented by the fact that until he faces the man who was not born of woman, he must 'bear-like' endure attacks by adversaries who cannot give him the *coup de grâce*. That can come from the mysterious person of the prophecy spoken by the apparition of the Bloody Child; at first confident that no such person could exist, he has learnt to fear the equivocation of the fiend whose lies are literally true; he is troubled by the increasing fear that at any moment any one of his adversaries may turn out to be the man whom he dreads. Every combat is therefore for him a matter of intolerable anxiety which gives place to relief. This happens in the encounter with Young Siward, whose death provokes the elated complacency of:

Thou wast born of woman.
But swords I smile at, weapons laugh to scorn,
Brandish'd by man that's of a woman born.

(v, vii, 11–13)

The moment of truth, both literally and metaphorically, comes when Macbeth is determined to go on and kill so long as opponents remain to be killed by him. In this mood

188

he is found by Macduff; yet he restrains himself from proceeding to what he securely feels sure is yet another victory;
his offer of mercy is rejected in a reply which tantalizingly
makes its full meaning clear only in its two last words.
Until these are spoken Macbeth must wait in suspense,
knowing what is coming, yet unable to believe that Macduff
is really saying what he says until it is said completely and
cannot be ignored.

> And let the angel whom thou still hast serv'd
> Tell thee Macduff was from his mother's womb
> Untimely ripp'd.

The consternation which Macbeth experiences as this reply
penetrates his complacency is summed up in his next speech.
There is rage as well as terror in 'Accursed be the tongue that
tells me so', and there is a recognition of his own cowardice,
which he seems incapable of overcoming, in 'it hath cow'd
my better part of man'. He is at last disillusioned of all faith
in the 'juggling fiends'; and in the shock of the revelation is
overwhelmed by all the fears hurrying back which the
'equivocations' had banished from his mind. And so he
refuses to fight. But Macduff's contemptuous exultation
with its threat of exhibiting him 'as our rarer monsters are'
stirs Macbeth's sense of shame; his soldier's pride returns,
his nobleman's sense of dishonour and indignity of being
exposed to the rabble as someone once feared but now to be
scorned. His courage returns; a real courage now, like that
which was described of him at the beginning of the play,
when he laughed at Fortune, and fought undismayed by
appalling odds. At last, horrible imaginings of how he would
be punished for the murder of Duncan—which have
tormented him since he conceived the murder, not merely
since carrying it out—are giving place to present fears; and
these he can face boldly. And so once again Macbeth can
disdain Fortune; even if Birnam Wood has come to Dunsi-
nane, and he is opposed by a man who is not of woman born,

he refuses to give credence to the prophecy until he has tried it; if Macduff kills him or he Macduff, then its truth or falsehood will be known and not till then. This is the way in which 'brave Macbeth' reacted once against Duncan's enemies when Fortune smiled on them. Now with grim humour born of fearlessness, for the joke is almost certainly at his own expense and he knows it, he cries, 'Yet I will try the last.' He will test in practice whether he can be killed or not. And the violence of his rush at Macduff expresses his determination to make the test a real one.

So much attention has been devoted to the part played by fear in Macbeth's emotional life because a sure foundation on which character can be built is provided once it has been realized that his objective includes the insistence on being safe. There are many other elements in Macbeth, but the aim here has been not to attempt to do the actor's work for him with an exhaustive analysis, but to give an example of what can be done with the text of one of Shakespeare's later plays where the unrealistic style is less obtrusive than in, say, *Romeo and Juliet*. Although rhetorical figures and images are not so disconcerting and are more obviously related to the dramatic growth of the action, the actor still derives help from considering them and their surface sense as a preliminary to making up his mind about emotions and objectives. The same kind of preparation will help to decide what is involved for Macbeth in his relationship with Banquo; here we find fear and resentment mixed with admission of the qualities which make Banquo the superior. But Macbeth's objective demands Banquo's death, for the great bond which must be cancelled ordains an arrangement (presumably made by Fortune) that Macbeth shall have no more than the use of what he has stolen in his own lifetime; that at some time after his death, Banquo's heirs will inherit the throne. It is impossible for Macbeth to consider Banquo without realizing that he himself has no children; and much of his torment comes from the knowledge that the witches have 'put a barren sceptre in my gripe'. To think of Banquo, too, means that Macbeth is tortured with the thought that unless he can change the course of events he has damned himself, doomed himself to punishment in the life to come merely to give the throne to Banquo's children; they will inherit, Macbeth thinks mistakenly, simply because he has interrupted the true succession. Again we find Banquo involved in Macbeth's emotions when we consider his despair. Fundamentally that derives from his subconscious knowledge, which often becomes conscious, that he cannot succeed in what he is doing, but that he cannot stop himself sinning in thought before the murder, nor can he repent after it. He is always driven onwards, once he has committed himself to action, by his objective of enjoying what was Duncan's, which presupposes safety.

I have not allowed courage to Macbeth, although he is spoken of as courageous at the beginning of the play: he is also spoken of as disdaining Fortune, but he does not disdain her in the action; similarly the action shows him full of fear except when the prophecies delude him into feeling safe, and when he faces 'present fears' and defies them in the last encounter with Macduff. The actor will also have to deal with Macbeth's cruel humour and his self-pity, both of which derive from his selfishness; it is unfair, he complains, that he could not say 'Amen', he had most need of pity; it is not fair that he should find himself exposed to the consequences of having murdered Duncan. Some examples of the humour have already been noticed, one more is worth attention:

> Be innocent of the knowledge, dearest chuck,
> Till thou applaud the deed.
>
> (III, ii, 45–46)

To be innocent of the knowledge is the only innocence that Lady Macbeth can have in this matter: for when she is no

191

longer ignorant of the knowledge once the deed has been done, the fact that she will applaud it will involve her in the guilt; then her innocence such as it has been, will have gone.

Although the picture which emerges of Macbeth is so black, it is still one which, in the circumstances imagined by Shakespeare, can evoke the pity necessary to tragedy. What Macbeth wants is, after all, in itself admirable. It is only possible for a man to want to be accepted as if he were Duncan when he himself is capable of evaluating Duncan at his true worth. A different kind of sinner would scorn all the virtues which he does not himself possess; but Macbeth, although poor in them, does not deny their essential richness. He can appreciate goodness. The pitiful thing about him is that he cannot earn the esteem he yearns for by the possession and exercise of the qualities which alone will give it to him for ever. He is caught in his own nature; it is his nature to admire worth, to want to be admired as worthy; but the only way which he can see open to him to win what he wants is one so full of violence and dangers that to tread it deprives him either of that admiration or of the ability to enjoy it (because he must feel safe); and in the end he has nothing.

The foregoing pages have been concerned with the process whereby an actor gains the intellectual knowledge of what it is that the character says, the sense of his lines, their implications, the emotions expressed, and the objective which makes the words necessary. About the second process, whereby he is able to feel these emotions and want these objectives, there is not much for me to say. The only point which must be made relates to what sometimes results from the way in which actors enable themselves to feel the emotions which they know intellectually the character feels. For instance, an actor will know easily enough that Oliver in *As You Like It* feels such a hatred for his younger brother that he wants Orlando murdered; the actor may still find himself unable to conceive how one brother could feel like this, and he may therefore find it impossible to feel truthfully the hatred which he must feel if he is to play Oliver's role. His preparation may therefore concern itself with imagining the gradual development of Oliver's hatred throughout the course of years. He will think of the father showing favouritism to Orlando, slighting the elder brother, of Orlando taking advantage of the situation; in order to create in himself the utterly false picture of Orlando which he thinks Oliver has, he may imagine Oliver giving credence to lies told him about the younger brother which seem to be confirmed by his superficial behaviour. By such methods the actor will be able to bring himself to the point at which he can feel truthfully the hatred which makes Oliver want his brother dead. And it is at this point that he must pause and carefully examine everything which Shakespeare lets him know about the character he has to play. In fact Shakespeare does not suggest any motive for Oliver's hatred; we are given merely Oliver hating his brother. The actor must therefore be careful not to assume that the reasons which he has imagined in order to feel the hatred himself are to become part of his presentation of the role; he has only to play Oliver as a man who hates his brother enough to plan his death, and not as a man who hates him to this extent from any of the motives which would be necessary before the actor could do such a thing. If an attempt is made to play the role with these motives, it will be the result of a confusion between the intellectual knowledge of what the character feels and wants, and the technique whereby an actor can make himself feel and want what he knows are the emotions and desires of the imaginary character.

With Shakespeare the actor needs to try to play the character in the circumstances of the play. And often these circumstances will direct our attention to the subtext, the life of the character that goes on beneath the sense of the text. It may be true that with other playwrights of later periods the text comes from the author, the subtext from the actor; but it seems to me that Shakespeare usually includes the subtext himself. He certainly has not given us the reason for Oliver's hatred of Orlando, so it may justifiably be argued that all the subtext must come from the actor. On the other hand, it is equally valid to reply that to play Oliver an actor merely needs to feel the hatred and want the objective without trying to play them as motivated in any particular way. The danger of assuming that all the subtext comes from the actor is illustrated easily enough in the case of Macbeth: Shakespeare has himself provided the key to Macbeth's emotions and objective. The text itself reveals the subtext by making it clear that Macbeth has a clarity of vision about good and evil which both incites him to and restrains him from the murder. Only by murder can he put himself in a position in which he will be treated as if he were of Duncan's calibre; but to murder Duncan will ensure judgement here. An actor who cannot feel himself capable of resolving to murder a man whose quality he evaluates so accurately may have to imagine motivations to give himself the resolution which are not Macbeth's motivations; but once the resolution is made it must be dissociated from the actor's motivations and transferred, as a reflex is conditioned, to those which he knows intellectually belong to Macbeth. If this is not done the actor will find himself inevitably trying to play one thing when Shakespeare's words make other demands on him.

The foregoing paragraph almost certainly will strike the reader as much more confident and dogmatic than the writer feels. Acting is so subtle and complex an activity that those of us who are not actors will do well to restrict ourselves to advice on those aspects of the art which are primarily concerned with gaining the necessary intellectual knowledge of a character which an actor can convert into a presentation of the role as if he were the very person come to life. But as it is often so difficult to gain that exact knowledge in practice there is a strong possibility that the modern actor will unconsciously and unintentionally take his way out of a difficulty by providing the character with a subtext which does not come from and is not implied by the text. For this reason the plea is made here, strongly but not complacently, that when a role is being prepared final decisions on the subtext might profitably be postponed until the text has been subjected to the kind of examination which has been outlined in the pages of this book. Of course, this may easily result in the actor merely deciding confidently to do exactly what had occurred to him spontaneously at his first glance at his part; for actors can often perceive swiftly and intuitively what critics and scholars can see only after much hard plodding.

GLOSSARY

ANADIPLOSIS: The beginning of a sentence, phrase, line or clause with the concluding word, or any prominent word, of the sentence, phrase, line or clause preceding.

ANTANACLASIS: The repetition of a word but with a different, if not a contrary, meaning.

ANTIMETABOLE: A figure in which the same words or ideas are repeated in inverse order.

ANTITHESIS: An opposition or contrast of ideas expressed by using as the corresponding members of two contiguous sentences or clauses words which are the opposite of, or are strongly contrasted with, each other.

BRACHYLOGIA: Conciseness of speech in which a number of nouns may be listed, and instead of each being connected separately with a verb as an independent sentence, the respective verbs are listed in the same order as the nouns to which each applies.

CLIMAX: A progression of thought through units of expression, each unit beginning with the word which ended the one preceding it.

EPANALEPSIS: A figure in which the same word or clause is repeated after intervening matter.

EPIZEUXIS: A figure in which a word is repeated but with vehemence or some other distinguishing emphasis.

OXYMORON: A figure in which contrary or incongruous terms are conjoined so as to give point to the statement: the giving of point by a statement which is literally impossible or absurd.

PARONOMASIA: A pun.

POLYPTOTON: The repetition of a word or phrase in the same sentence in different inflexions or cases. A repetition of words derived from the same etymological root.

SYNOECIOSIS: The association or coupling with one another of contrasted or heterogenous ideas or things.

ZEUGMA: A figure in which one word is made to refer to more than one of a sentence.

INDEX

Actor, An Excellent, 94ff.

Baker, Sir Richard, 96f.
Baldwin, T. W., 9, 10, 50
Brinsley, R., 8, 9, 11–14
Bulwer, J., 83; *Chirologia,* 86f., 98, 100ff.; *Chironomia,* 85, 98–100ff.

Character, xix, 82ff., 140ff.; and poetry, xixf., 1ff., 6ff., 18f., 22f., 53f., 55ff., 111ff., 190
Characters (from Shakespeare), Henry V, 3f., 18f., 29, 52f.; Juliet, 49f., 117ff.; Lawrence, Friar, 122ff.; Macbeth, 18f., 45, 75f., 78f., 108f., 163ff., 194; Oliver (*As You Like It*), 192ff.; Romeo, 116ff.
Clemen, W. H., 153ff., 159, 161

Emotion, 86ff., 129ff.
Enthemyme, 50ff.
Epaminondas, 77

Flecknoe, R., 92, 95f.
Francis of Assisi, St., 123, 128f., 131
Fraunce, A., 7, 12, 13, 20ff.

Gifford, H., 77

Hall, J., 182
Heywood, T., 16, 17, 92
Hopton, R., 92

Identification, 89ff., 92
Imagery, 78ff., 152ff.

Kempe, W., 7, 12

Leach, A. F., 8
Literary Criticism, and acting, 124ff., 152ff.

Mermaid Theatre, 98ff.
Miles, Bernard, 98ff.
Miriam Joseph, Sister, 50
Mulcaster, R., 10, 16

Objective, 110ff.
Obscurity, 70ff.
Oratory, and acting, 93ff.

Palsgrave, J., 16
Patterns, balanced, 40ff., 49, 137ff. 167, 169
Puttenham, G., 4, 21ff., 30

Rhetoric, and dramatic writing, 5; the figures of, – (i) of sentence, 7f., 12ff., 48f.; (ii) of words, – *anadiplosis,* 25; *antanaclasis,* 3f., 32f.; *antimetabole,* 25f.; *antithesis,* xixf., 35ff., 104ff., 144, 167; *brachylogia,* 42f.; *climax,* 21ff.; *epanalepsis,* 26ff.; *epizeuxis,* 28f.; *oxymoron,* 39; *paradox,* 39; *paronomasia,* 3, 29ff., 167; *polyptoton,* 33ff.; *prosonomasiae,* see *paronomasia*; *synoeciosis,* 38; *zeugma,* 41f.; pronunciation, 8ff., 20ff., 46ff.; and modern acting, 83ff.; tropes, 6f., 12ff., 46f.